The Beauty Industry

The beauty industry is now a multinational, multi-million dollar business. In recent years its place in contemporary culture has altered hugely as salons have become not simply places to have a hair cut or your nails done, but increasingly sites of physical and even emotional therapy. In this fascinating and nuanced study, Paula Black strips away many popular assumptions about the beauty industry, including the one that says it exploits people's insecurity by projecting an illusory beauty myth. The interviews in this book – both with the beauty industry's workers and its clients – reveal a far more complex and interesting picture, and, in their presentation, Black reformulates many feminist debates around choice and constraint. The debates addressed include issues around the body; the construction and maintenance of gender identity; changing definitions of health and well being; and labour processes.

Paula Black is a Lecturer in Sociology at the University of Sussex.

The Beauty Industry

Gender, culture, pleasure

Paula Black

Routledge
Taylor & Francis Group

LONDON AND NEW YORK

First published 2004
by Routledge
2 Park Square, Milton Park, Abingdon, Oxon, OX14 4RN

Simultaneously published in the USA and Canada
by Routledge
270 Madison Ave, New York, NY 10016

Transferred to Digital Printing 2005

Routledge is an imprint of the Taylor & Francis Group

© 2004 Paula Black

Typeset in Bembo and Gill by BC Typesetting Ltd, Bristol
Printed and bound in Great Britain by
TJI Digital, Padstow, Cornwall

British Library Cataloguing in Publication Data
A catalogue record for this book is available from the British Library

Library of Congress Cataloging in Publication Data
A catalog record for this book has been requested

ISBN 0–415–32158–1 (hbk)
ISBN 0–415–32157–3 (pbk)

For Pamela Black and in memory of Rudy Black

Contents

Acknowledgements

As books take so long to write and research it is tempting to list all of those who have been involved in any small way. In order to avoid these acknowledgements reading like an Oscar winner's acceptance speech I will inevitably miss some who have helped and supported me along the way. I can only apologise for this. I should first mention my editors at Routledge, Mari Shullaw and Gerhard Boomgarten, who have offered invaluable advice. Colleagues in the departments of sociology at the University of Derby and the University of Manchester have provided a stimulating academic context. In the short time I have been based at the University of Sussex, I have also received nothing but kindness and academic support. In addition, staff and Ph.D. students at the Institute of Women, Gender and Development Studies, Ahfad University for Women, Sudan, have been an inspiration.

Particular appreciation is reserved for the constructive criticism provided by those readers who have ploughed through sections of this book. Thanks to Joanne Hollows, Mary Holmes, Ursula Sharma and Gary Hazeldine. Ann Akeroyd also provided invaluable references which have improved my understanding of some of the issues I discuss.

The fieldwork for this book has been carried out over an extended period of time, and I am immensely grateful to Ursula Sharma and Mary Madden who conducted some of the interviews and contributed their understanding and insight. I have obtained permission from Mary and Ursula to interpret the material they generated in my own way, but both have had an input into the research process. Funding for part of this process was provided by the Faculty of Social Sciences and Law, University of Manchester.

The following people have made the book-writing process more enjoyable and generally improved my life in all kinds of ways: Gary Hazeldine, Francis Lawn, Rachel Grellier, Ursula Sharma, Gareth Twose, Wolfgang Weber, Simon Speck, Holly Huber, Richard Scott, Nicola Coxon, David Davidson, Sheree Cross, Paul Keleman, Emerson Daniel, Jae Charles, Bridget Byrne.

Finally, my eternal gratitude lies with the beauty therapists and clients who agreed to take part in this research. There was very little reward involved in their giving up valuable time to talk to me. That they did so is a testament to the immense tolerance people still seem to have for an inquisitive sociologist. Thanks then to all of the staff in the beauty therapy department at 'Northern College', all of the beauty therapists interviewed in the two sites, and the clients I have quoted here.

Parts of Chapter 4 were originally published with Ursula Sharma in *Sociology* 35, 4: 913–931 (2001).

Chapter 1

'Ordinary people come through here'

Introducing the work of the beauty salon

Yvette owns a beauty salon in a small city in the UK. This salon caters predominantly to white women who do not have access to large amounts of disposable income. Yvette is adamant that visits to salons are a necessary and pleasurable part of a woman's life.

> I mean we still get ladies in who say 'Oh I can't afford that'. My answer is well, I ask them a question, 'Has he [husband] got a football season ticket?' and if she says 'Yes', 'Well, spend an equal amount of money on your face', and then they see it in a different light. Because the man is a bit old-fashioned, you know, 'Spending all that money on your face, you can't see what's happened'.
>
> (Yvette BT)

The discussion from which this quote is taken arose during a period I spent at Yvette's in the run-up to Christmas. During this time my role was to offer glasses of sherry and mince pies to the women coming into the salon for pre-holiday treatments. The conversation among these women, fuelled a little by the sherry, turned to relationships with men and their views about the amount of time and money women spend on their bodies. The general feeling was that men did not understand the benefits of beauty salon treatments or the effort that went into maintaining a feminine appearance. Yvette herself points out how many men come into the salon at that time of year in order to purchase gift vouchers for wives and girlfriends. She says that the discomfort experienced by older men in particular at having to enter the doors of the salon is often covered by a course humour. Some men refer to gift vouchers as 'scaffolding and filling vouchers'. This misunderstanding and the guilt some women feel about spending time and money in the salon gave rise to Yvette's comment above. During the course of this research I spent much time with Yvette and her employees and she never once wavered in her belief in the value of the beauty salon, while at the same time maintaining a healthy scepticism about the more ambitious claims made for some treatments.

During the past few years in every town I have visited, in every part of the world, I have looked in beauty salon windows, received beauty treatments and collected endless price lists for a huge variety of treatments. Yet before I began research into beauty therapy I had never entered a beauty salon; in fact I hardly noticed their existence. The research in the area began accidentally while I was involved in a different research project. Despite being a regular purchaser of beauty products and a self-critical mirror gazer, my feminist politics allowed only a deep suspicion of the activities of the beauty industry. Perhaps due to the legacy of early 1980s feminism with which I grew up, I felt that too heavy an investment in femininity through beauty treatments was somehow a betrayal of my own political beliefs. To some extent I still believe this, and I devote much space in this book to understanding women's use of beauty salons from a feminist position. However, I have also learned much about what actually goes on behind the closed doors of beauty salons. As Yvette remarked to me, 'Ordinary people come through here'. The desire of these 'ordinary people' is for pleasure and escapism. They wish to 'make the best of themselves'. They enjoy the atmosphere of a feminised space in the company of other women. They are also unconcerned with beauty. The practices and discourses which intersect in the salon are varied and complex. So this book is not concerned with beauty *per se*; rather it is an investigation of what is termed 'the beauty industry' through the specific context of the beauty salon. Although both of these subjects contain beauty in their title, my concern has been to reflect the interests of the clients and therapists in beauty salons, and their experiences cannot be reduced to the catch-all phrase of 'beauty'.

The beauty salon

It seems inappropriate to continue with a discussion of the beauty salon without first describing the social space I am focusing upon. A beauty salon has its own ambience. The uniforms of the staff, the decor, the layout, reflect the aspirations of the owner. Some salons give the immediate impression of a clinic where staff dress in white, and where formality is emphasised. These white overalls offer the impression of both cleanliness and clinicisation. They emphasise the medicalised nature of some of the treatments available, as well as the claims to professional status of the staff. In other salons, the staff are required to dress in more flamboyant colours, often matched by the decor and the welcome received by the client. Clothing colours other than white subtly alter the ambience of the salon and the message sent out to clients. Pastel shades are equated with femininity and with friendliness. These are, of course, associated. More contemporary, bolder shades convey a modern salon and a gender neutrality which encourages a specific female clientele, as well as male clients. Walls are decorated with the qualification certificates of staff and membership certificates of professional organisations. Salons generally contain a waiting area with comfortable seating and assorted magazines. These magazines will vary with the clientele of the salon but mainstream women's magazines such as *Marie Claire* or *Cosmopolitan* are examples. Celebrity magazines such as *Hello* or *OK* are also popular. The entrance area will also contain a till close to the door where clients are taken after their treatment; a private area for staff; bathroom facilities; screened cubicles or private rooms where treatments are carried out; and if the salon offers nail treatments, there is also a more communal treatment area where manicures are performed (interestingly, in the UK pedicures are performed in the private cubicles). The salon has its own routines and invisible tracks along which staff walk in greeting clients, guiding them to treatment rooms, offering refreshments, and finally leading to the point where payment is made. Salons have their own smell which is that of the equipment and chemicals used for treatments, intermingled with the pleasant aromas of perfumed creams and lotions, cups of tea and coffee, and sometimes too the strong smell of nail products. It is in this atmosphere that the intimate routines of body maintenance are carried out.

This template relates most closely to the case of the UK. In countries around the world the salon varies in order to accommodate localised beauty practices and traditions. In the USA and Caribbean certain treatments are received in communal areas with only those which require exposure of the body necessitating movement to private screened spaces. I once spent more than three hours in a salon in Kingston, Jamaica, while false nails were applied to my fingers. During this time as I sat in the communal area in this small, local salon I had time to chat to the regular clients also receiving treatments. Other shopkeepers came in to talk and to deliver cold drinks requested by the clients. I was able to spend uninterrupted time talking to a relative who had accompanied me on the trip. During the whole of this period there was no time that conversation was not going on between shifting groups of women. At the same time a Hollywood film played continuously on video in the corner. While I was present it began three times under the disinterested gaze of the clients.

In Sudan, traditional salons contain a collective seating area where women sit to talk and receive treatments. In this area, beautiful and elaborate designs in henna are applied to the hands and feet of married women. Single women are allowed only one hand or foot to be decorated in this fashion. A separate area of the salon accommodates a specific type of smoke-based sauna where individual women sit under cloth covers to receive this treatment, away from the communal areas. The heady, musky smell of the smoke permeates the salon, and lingers on the clothes and hair of all who have been present. This smell, when applied directly to the body in this ritualised sauna treatment, signifies preparation for sex with the husband. In this way preparation for sex with a male partner occurs in the company of other women. As more modern salons arrive in Sudan, these local beauty practices have been accommodated into a contemporary and internationalised design. So, for example, hairdressing and beauty treatments are carried out in a large communal space as in salons in the USA, but a small room is set aside for married women to receive their henna treatment. In this way we can see that the international beauty industry is modified at a local level to incorporate specific cultural practices. This in turn affects the types of relationships which develop within the confines of the salon.

Beauty therapy is part of a vast multinational industry. This industry includes cosmetics and skin care products, beauty treatments in spas, gyms, hotels and holiday resorts and salons; an advertising industry which supports this consumption; the cosmetic surgery industry; hair care; the dieting industry, and so on. The value of the professional beauty industry in the UK in 1998 was £366 million, which represented a growth of almost 6 per cent on the previous year (Guild News, 1999). This figure includes beauty therapy treatments in a variety of sites including mobile, hair and beauty salons and health clubs, as well as the conventional beauty salon. In the UK in 2002 there were almost 6.4 million users of beauty salons, an increase of 17 per cent on the previous year (Guild News, 2002). In 2000 the numbers of men using salons in the UK stood at 70,000 (Guild News, 2001). The age range of all clients in 2002 was 18 to 30 (22 per cent); 30 to 45 (4 per cent); 45-plus (36 per cent). This figure comes from an official beauty industry guild, and I find the fact that under-eighteens are not mentioned a little surprising, since therapists have mentioned to me that younger clients do visit salons. In 2002 in the UK the proportion of business type was as follows: high street salon 41 per cent; home-based salon 27 per cent; hairdressing and beauty 10 per cent; health club 7 per cent; mobile 10 per cent and nails/other 5 per cent. Between 2001 and 2002 there was a growth of 22 per cent in the number of businesses in the beauty sector. This increase follows growth in previous years (Guild News, 2002). The increase in business is due partly to the expanded repertoire of treatments available. Salons now not only offer the standard manicures, facials, waxing and electrolysis, but may additionally offer aromatherapy, massage, reflexology and reiki. Despite this diversity the most popular treatments remain waxing and manicures. However, as use of the beauty industry in all its forms has rocketed, measured levels of satisfaction that individuals feel with their bodies and their looks have decreased (Synnott, 1993).

Do beauty salons matter?

Why does beauty matter? Beauty flies in the face of a puritanical utilitarianism. It defies the reductiveness of both the political left and the political right in their efforts to bend it to a mission. Beauty subverts dogma by activating the realm of fantasy and imagination. It reminds us that the enjoyment of 'mere' pleasure is an important element of our humanity. And it knits the mind and body together at a time when they seem all too easily divided.

(Brand, 2000, p. xv)

Beauty has been the subject of much debate and conjecture for centuries. It has been a key issue in a range of fields from art theory to philosophy. Politics, art and philosophy may interlink through work on beauty, as, for example, in the work of the performance artist Orlan. She has undergone a series of cosmetic surgery procedures on her face, each time filming the procedures and offering a commentary during the operation (Brand, 2000). Her intention has been to take features of significance from works of art and transplant them on to and into her own face. Beauty too is routinely associated not simply with external appearance but also with positive attributes such as morality and kindness. However, it is not in this sense that I am concerned with beauty here.

The types of salons in which I have conducted my research and drawn my interviewees from range from the city centre branch of a large multinational, through the small local salon catering to white working-class women, to those salons situated in a middle-class area of a large city. Wherever possible, I have also visited salons around the world. What all of these salons have in common, however, is that they are part of the everyday routines of their clients. They offer services which are discreet and professional. These places are not the Los Angeles salons populated by TV stars and the very wealthy. The requests for 'Brazilian' bikini line waxes, while not uncommon, do not form the main focus of the business of these salons. At the time of writing, a programme called *The Salon* recently aired on Channel 4 on UK TV. This is another 'reality' documentary showing life in a hair and beauty salon. While I recognise the disagreements, and sometimes camaraderie, among the staff, much of the rest of the programme is unrecognisable in relation to the salons I have visited. TV portrays clients and workers as idiosyncratic, highly fashionable young gossip-mongers. In contrast, I wish to paint a picture of the salon showing how 'ordinary people come through here'. The clients in this study were generally not high spenders on salon treatments. Although, if taken together, spending on beauty items, hairdressing and salon treatments could form a significant percentage of their disposable income, all managed their budgets carefully. The cost of treatments remained an issue for all of those interviewed. Despite this fact, where treatments were seen as a necessity money would always be found. In order to understand the role of the salon in women's lives it is important to place it in the context of women's experience:

> When women put on a face, they continue to express ideas of naturalness and artifice, authenticity and deception, propriety and danger, modernity and tradition. Making up remains a gesture bound to perceptions of self and body, the intimate and the social – a gesture rooted in women's everyday lives.
>
> (Peiss, 1998, p. 270)

These claims are true of using make-up, and they are true of beauty treatments more generally, including visits to the beauty salon. Inside the beauty salon a world exists, which, although closed and intimate, is also open to the influences of the wider world within which the salon is situated. These enclosed social worlds have long drawn the attention of ethnographers and sociologists.

However, in 1976, Lofland could claim authoritatively that feminised spaces in particular had been overlooked in the development of social theorising:

> As far as I know, for example, there is not a single published study of a beauty parlour, a setting in which many women may undoubtedly develop close and meaningful relationships.
>
> (Lofland, 1976, p. 154)

The attention of earlier ethnographers had indeed been drawn by the social spaces and intimate worlds open to men. The world of the beauty salon, the hairdressing salon, the launderette, has received much less attention. Julie Willett, for example, claims:

> For my grandmother and many of her friends and relatives, the church, the front porch, and the beauty shop were part of a larger women's culture that provided an invaluable source of information and the same types of social networks that historians have been so willing to see in saloons and other all-male institutions.
>
> (Willett, 2000, p. 2)

This omission has been for several reasons. First, and most obviously, because many of the researchers discussed in the sociological textbooks outlining this form of research, or the historians mentioned by Willett, are themselves male. Researchers will always choose to work in those areas where their access and their 'performance' in the research role is made easiest. Second, male worlds have stood for social worlds in general. The world of the street corner, the poolhall or the medical training school have been written about as if they were gender-neutral spaces. Third, an uneasy relationship exists between empirically grounded research and more theoretically orientated work. This uneasy relationship within British academia has seen a general elevation of theoretical research and publications. Those involved in empirical research have also at times derided theory without empirical groundings. If ethnographic studies have been wary of the role of grand-scale theory, and in turn theorists have often been dismissive of 'mere empiricism', then gender simply adds to these difficulties. I do not intend to go into the history of the debates between qualitative researchers, quantitative researchers and theorists around epistemology and methodology, suffice to say that it is predominantly in feminist debates of the past twenty years or so where gender has served as a key factor. The work of Dorothy Smith (1987), for example, may be seen as a major intervention into this area, and an argument for the possibility of grounding social theorising in the 'everyday world' of women.

The question of masculine representations cannot be disentangled from the question of 'race'. Male researchers have provided us with a rich and vivid description of the world of men at the same time as white researchers have provided us with views of racially specific social worlds. If in 1976 when Lofland was writing, gender had not been foregrounded as important in empirical studies, then this was even more the case with race. As Willett points out at the same time as she is criticising the masculinist bias of historical studies, the world inhabited by her grandmother was exclusively white. Indeed, the small Midwestern town in the USA she inhabited could boast that neither a 'catholic or a "nigger" had ever spent the night in the town' (Willett, 2000, p.2). What is striking about so much of the recent research into beauty culture, however, is how this question of 'race' is foregrounded. Willett shows how this sense of whiteness is an important aspect of identity for the women in the beauty salons in that small town.

These omissions have to some extent been corrected in more recent research. A number of studies in a variety of countries have focused upon such spaces. One review, for example, boasts the impressive title 'The great good place – cafes, coffee shops, community centers, beauty parlours, general stores, bars, hangouts, and how they get you through the day' (Oldenburg and Hummon, 1991). In specific relation to beauty and hairdressing salons, there has been a proliferation of studies. Some of these have looked at the history and workings of the beauty industry *per se* (Peiss, 1998; Willett, 2000; Gimlin, 2002) or at the development of

African-American beauty businesses and aesthetics (Rooks, 1998; Craig, 2002). Others have produced ethnographic studies of specific locations (Gimlin, 1996; Furman, 1997; Thompson, 1998). Tangentially, significant areas of research have also grown up around the politics of body hair (Synnott, 1987; Basow, 1991; Zdatny, 1993; Tiggermann and Kenyon, 1998; Herzig, 1999; Lawson, 1999); psychological studies into the effects of physical attractiveness (Webster and Driskell, 1983; Kyle and Mahler, 1996); studies of beauty pageants (Cohen *et al.*, 1995; Craig, 2002); work on cosmetic surgery (Davis, 1995; Haiken, 1997; Gilman, 1999; Negrin, 2002); and economic assessments of the effects of looks upon career prospects and earning potential (Hamermesh and Biddle, 1994; Averett and Korenman, 1995).

The beauty salon stands at the intersection of a number of techniques of the body (Mauss, 1973) which in turn relate to gender, the body, sexuality, class, commodification, leisure practices, consumption and so on. As such it is a useful and important microcosm of wider social relationships. A variety of studies around the world now attest to the importance of this area of research. What these various studies show is that while each individual salon contains characteristics specific to that location or culture, there are key themes common to these studies. First, the salon may be seen as a relatively homogeneous space in terms of the gender and ethnicity of the clients. Salons tend to cater to a specific clientele in relation to both ethnicity and gender. Salons are, of course, overwhelmingly female spaces. Where men are present they are there as an almost invisible minority, or are deliberately targeted as a consumer base by the policy of the salon. Such targeting will affect the ambience, treatments offered and décor of the salon. Where men are not seen as a core clientele, the salon remains a space for the construction and maintenance of femininity and reflects these activities. In a similar vein, ethnicity is also worked upon and reinforced in the salon. In the UK local salons in particular are divided into those catering to white women, African-Caribbean salons, and those serving an Asian clientele. The larger, city centre chains may be less segmented, although this is generally the case. Salons are also largely segmented along class lines. The salon will tailor its services and prices to the socio-economic status of its customers. In this way the salon both reflects and reinforces divisions along gender, ethnicity and class lines. All studies of salons take this wider social context into account.

Linked to this segmentation is the body-work which occurs in the salon. Here, the body is moulded and worked on in order to achieve a look, and sometimes also a feeling, which is regarded as 'appropriate' in relation to categories of gender, age, sexuality, class and ethnicity. The therapist and the client work together in order to maintain a sense of what is 'appropriate' or 'acceptable' or even 'normal' for the woman. This is a highly complex and carefully negotiated process and I return to it in a detailed discussion in Chapter 3.

Next, all salons entail the management of relationships between staff and clients. The therapist attempts to assert her professional status and expertise, and the client expects a service for which she is paying. The power balance between the two depends upon this combination of professional expertise, commodified relationship, and also the level of personal intimacy between client and therapist. The therapists in my study all claimed that one of their functions was to offer counselling in their relationships with clients. Although clients access the salon for a specific treatment, part of the experience they desire is to be listened to and to be able to off-load emotional issues in a relationship which, while often bearing a superficial resemblance to friendship, is actually a carefully managed piece of emotional labour. The client does not feel she needs to reciprocate, and the therapist views this counselling as a vital part of her role. The relationships between clients and therapists are also cut across by inequalities in education, income and in some cases also ethnicity.

Finally, the services offered in the salon and the relationships between clients and therapists may be more or less commodified. The beauty salon is after all a business venture and, while guided by professional ethics, the motivation is profit. The beauty industry itself may be understood in relation to consumption practices and processes of exchange. While focusing on the relationships of friendship and intimacy which may form within the salon, it is also important to maintain an awareness of the economic base to the activities being carried out there. This commodification of body practices is a theme to which I return throughout this book.

Researching the beauty salon

The material contained in this book is based on a multi-method piece of research. The main source of data is interviews with eighteen beauty therapists and teachers of beauty therapy as well as with twenty-three clients of beauty salons. One beauty therapist spoke extensively of her experiences as a client, although she has been categorised as a therapist. All interviews were in-depth and detailed. Clients were asked to complete a short questionnaire detailing biographical information and the extent of their salon use. In addition to this material I have spent time in salons, observing and sometimes participating in the activities going on there. I have also spent time in a college where beauty therapy is taught, speaking to both staff and students, and focus groups have been conducted with these members of staff. The literature of professional associations has been studied, and interviews were also conducted with key officials in these associations. Not least, I have received a variety of treatments in a range of salons.

Interviewees were recruited by a variety of methods. Teachers of beauty therapy were all based in one college and they in turn put me in touch with other therapists whom they knew. In addition, salons were approached directly by letter or personal visits. All salons were based either in a large city in the North of England, or a smaller city in the English Midlands. In the smaller city a great deal of leg work was used to visit as many salons as possible to recruit salon staff and clients to the research. Care was taken to ensure a diversity of salon types. In the larger city the local telephone directory was used to send a letter to all salons in the area. All were then contacted by telephone and those who agreed to participate were visited in person. In addition, in both sites, women attending keep fit classes in local sport centres were also approached. In this way sample variety was ensured, although in no way could this group of women be regarded as reliably representative of all salon clients and therapists. All the beauty therapists were heterosexual, and aged between their early twenties and early fifties. One therapist was African-Caribbean, and all the others were white British.

All clients reported that they were heterosexual, and sixteen were in a relationship at the time of interview. Nine of the women had children. The clients' ages ranged from 21 to 75, with the majority clustered in the thirties range. The vast majority were in paid employment, and all had worked outside of the home at some point. At the time of interview, seventeen were working full-time. The remainder either worked part-time or were students, one woman was unemployed, one was not working due to ill-health and one woman had retired. The types of employment they were engaged in varied, although, as would be expected with a female sample, there was a predominance of service sector and professional occupations. There was also a variation in highest qualification, ranging from four women who held no formal qualifications through to an M.Sc. Eight clients held degrees. Almost all of the sample were white British, with two women describing themselves as black African-Caribbean, and one as Indian.

I have used a variety of methods to analyse this varied material, but I have focused predominantly on the interviews. These were transcribed in full and read through thoroughly several times. All were then coded in order to identify themes and issues contained within them. Although this coding introduces some level of interpretation I tried to remain as close to the data as possible at this stage. In presenting the findings of this analysis, I can only argue for the most convincing and appropriate explanations as I see them. My broad theoretical framework for interpreting this vast wealth of material has been eclectic and I have selected theorists of class, gender and 'race' where these have seemed useful. However, in this eclecticism I have avoided epistemological contradictions. In particular, I have maintained an analysis which allows us to acknowledge the view from women's lives, without having to accept that experience necessarily guarantees expertise on a subject:

What is the relationship between experience and knowledge for the standpoint theories? I stressed earlier that what 'grounds' feminist standpoint theory is not women's experiences but the view from women's lives . . . we can all learn about our own lives at the center of the social order if we start our thought from the perspective of lives at the margins.

(Harding, 1991, p. 269)

Harding makes an important distinction between experiences as privileged data, and the view from a particular position. In viewing women's lives as at the margins of the social order, we can begin to rethink the particular subject of enquiry by starting from this location. However, the interpretation of this view is key. Unmediated, 'authentic' experience is a fallacy. Privileged access to some essential truth is also a fallacy. As a sociologist I have listened, read and interpreted from a sociological viewpoint, and I believe it is the responsibility of the researcher to admit bravely to her analysis rather than to claim a simple representation of the research area. In each of the following chapters I have tried to make clear my own interpretations of the data generated, and to place myself firmly within the text.

What happens in the beauty salon?

Charlotte provides a good basis upon which to build a clear picture of what the beauty therapist actually does:

Interviewer (I): Why do you think people visit salons?
Charlotte (BT): To make themselves feel better. To enhance what is already there so that doesn't mean that they have to go for surgery, it's just, for example, they can't be bothered to be cut so they just have their eyelashes tinted. Its making more of a definition of what's there. Pampering, a luxury − a lot of them [clients] think it's a luxury. A lot of people think it's a necessity depending on which treatment, for example, electrolysis. It's a necessity to some of our clients. And I think just for a chat, and to offload.

All clients in the salon have one 'thing' which is important to them, and which prompts their salon visits. They may undertake other treatments in addition to this core treatment but, when time or money restricts the potential for salon visits, these other subsidiary experiences may be shed. If a woman visits a salon for a treatment which is important to her, then this becomes interwoven with her biography and is not to be dismissed lightly. It is also important to note the different types of treatments available in salons, and the different roles they play in women's own experiences. The fragmented nature of beauty therapy means that a large range of treatments are available and that women may be present in the salon for differing reasons, and receive very different experiences. One woman undertaking aromatherapy massage in order to feel 'nurtured' explains her salon use very differently to the woman who returns regularly for a half-hour painful leg wax seen as necessary in her terms to appear groomed and fully feminine. The combination of different treatment types varies according to each client, and may also change throughout the lifecourse. Therapists at times receive treatments themselves and practice treatments on each other. Although in this study I have clearly demarcated client/therapist, in reality some blurring exists. I have divided treatments into four types based on the testimonies of clients: pampering, regular grooming, health treatments and corrective treatments. In addition, the area of 'counselling' is important to therapists when describing the work they do.

Pampering

It is perhaps in the area of pampering that we encounter most clearly the image of the beauty salon. Pampering is seen to be a corollary of beauty. There is a hint of luxury, indulgence and vanity around pampering treatments. Beauty therapists make a distinction between the types of women who enter the salon for pampering treatments. Those women who do not engage in paid employment, and who nevertheless enjoy a high level of income, are sometimes described as 'ladies who lunch'. They are regular visitors to their chosen salon which is often situated in a predominantly middle-class area, and where prices are slightly higher than might be charged by salons catering to a less affluent clientele.

It is, however, a second group of women who are more often consumers of the pampering experience. These are women whose time is divided between family life, paid employment and social activities. To be pampered is to treat yourself, to take time out, and to indulge in luxury. Pampering is not about necessity but about desire. It is also about escape. Pampering treatments include pedicures, facials and massages. They are less likely to include more painful treatments such as waxing or electrolysis, although this may be the case where the time for oneself is the luxury rather than the treatment. For clients who come to the salon to be pampered the ambience is vital. The salon must be welcoming, friendly, warm, and above all clean. The client needs to feel comfortable and special enough to justify the economic outlay she is making. A very delicate balance must be achieved before the woman will attend the salon for pampering. She must feel that she needs time to herself, that she deserves this time, and that she can justify the expense. Once these conditions are in place the salon and the therapist must suit her requirements and she must set aside the time required for the visit. I return to the role of pampering treatments in Chapter 3 where they are understood in relation to debates around the political economy of time.

Routine grooming

Routine visits to the beauty salon relate to grooming. These beauty treatments are regarded either as a necessity or at least a routine part of body maintenance. Specific grooming treatments maintain the body and appearance of the client to a desired appropriate standard. Routine treatments by their very nature are less related to pleasure and escapism and more to the functional achievement of the minimum standards of bodily appearance. This is one explanation for the increasing numbers of men in salons. Grooming for men includes manicures, facials and waxing of unwanted body hair on back, chest and shoulders and, since these treatments may be explained in terms of 'looking after myself' or as male grooming, they do not carry the feminised associations inherent in other types of 'beauty' treatments. Despite this functional priority for routine treatments the time spent in the salon, the experience during the treatment, or its effects may also be perceived as pleasurable by the client. Functionality does not necessarily exclude pleasure. If pampering relates to a discourse of stress, 'time for myself' or 'I deserve it' justifications, grooming treatments are seen more as necessities which require less justification. Where explanation is sought it is often received in terms of an 'acceptable' standard of appearance within the workplace. I detail the role of grooming in the working lives of clients in Chapter 4.

Health treatments

Practices in the salon which are described as 'health treatments' may be further divided into those which are accessed in order to alleviate the symptoms of medically recognised illnesses, and those which the clients describe as contributing to a more general and holistic sense of well-being. Although there is of course some overlap between the treatments, the justifications for both are explained differently. The types of clients and the role that their salon visits play in their lives also vary according to whether their health treatments are related to chronic ill-health, or engaged in for the pursuit of 'well-being'. In order to understand health treatments for those who do not have any medically recognised illness, I refer to the concept of the healthy lifestyle. In doing so I am able to link together leisure activities, consumption practices and health. In addition, beauty therapy exists in relationship to the medical profession and complementary therapies, and therapists themselves emphasise the health aspects of their work in order to boost their own professional status. I return to the role of health treatments in the lives of clients and therapists in Chapter 5.

Corrective

The final group of treatments, or ways in which women account for their salon visits, is in terms of corrective procedures. There is little evidence here that the client is drawn to pleasure. Rather, corrective treatments are aimed at producing what is regarded as 'normal'. Electrolysis for the removal of facial hair is an example of this treatment type. The client who attends for corrective procedures is less likely to discuss her salon use, instead remaining secretive and often embarrassed. Facial hair acts as a signifier of masculinity and, in order to return to a 'normal' female state, treatment is required.

These women then are not dealing in vanity or aiming for beauty; instead their desire is not to be noticed. This area of treatment in particular throws into relief the work that must be done to police the boundaries of feminine normality and the artifice of such a supposedly natural state. Although the time spent in the salon here is certainly about time for the self, it is seen as an absolute necessity rather than a treat or a luxury. Corrective treatments share some similarities with health treatments aimed at alleviating the symptoms of chronic conditions, in that the women who undertake them claim to reject any notion of pleasure for its own sake; rather their treatment is seen to feed into more important and more necessary aspects of their lives.

Counselling

In addition to the types of treatments outlined by clients, the beauty therapists claimed to fulfil a counselling role in the salon. The role of therapist is as unofficial counsellor rather than participant in a general conversation. Beauty therapists must carry out both body and emotion work. They provide a listening service to their clients and form relationships which, although more distant than friendships, are more intimate than those formed in other service sectors. This is perhaps comparable to the relationships between clients and hairdressers or complementary therapists.

This counselling role was an ambiguous experience for the therapists. Although they were aware of the benefits to the client, and of the fact that this was one of the key motivating reasons for women to return for treatment, in terms of their own mental and emotional health, this role was a difficult and sometimes exhausting experience. At the same time they also derived immense personal satisfaction from having helped and listened to clients (Sharma and Black, 1999). I will return to this claim in more depth in Chapter 4 where I discuss emotional labour in the work of the therapist.

The structure of the book

In the following chapters I set out the world of the beauty salon and focus on one particular aspect of its work in detail. I draw extensively on interview material, and all quotes are referenced according to names I have given to interviewees. Beauty therapist respondents are given a name followed by the initials BT in order to distinguish their comments from those of clients. In Chapter 2 I outline the history of the beauty industry, paying particular attention to the USA. Chapter 3 forms the core of the book. Here I present the key findings from the interviews and lay out the analytical structure for making sense of women's use of beauty salons. In Chapter 4 I turn to what I have called the 'hidden labour of beauty'. Here I investigate both the role of emotional labour in the work of the beauty therapist and also the role that salon treatments play in the employment lives of salon clients. Chapter 5 focuses on the health-related claims made for beauty therapy. The discussion is divided into two sections. In the first section I examine the health-related treatments used by beauty salon clients. I place these treatments in the context of definitions of what it means to be healthy and the competing analyses of the role of medicine in contemporary society. In particular I focus on the concept of the healthy lifestyle as a means of tying together consumption practices, health, and beauty treatments. In the second section I investigate the health-related role of the therapist and her relationship with the medical profession and complementary therapies. Any of these chapters may be read in isolation. Due to the fragmented nature of the beauty industry, and the many types of treatments offered in the salon, it is possible to focus on one particular area. However, Chapter 3 sets out much of the empirical and analytical material which provides a framework for this focus.

Chapter 2

Inventing beauty

The history of the beauty salon

The beauty industry is not a historically recent phenomenon. Throughout history, women and men have used creams, lotions and preparations to alter their bodies in order to conform to the aesthetic standards of their day and their social position. However, the contemporary beauty industry, and the beauty salon upon which I shall focus, has its roots in the mid-nineteenth century from which time we can trace advertising aimed at women. We can also see the development of businesses based upon the marketing of beauty products, and the treatment of clients. Following this period there is also a clear development of a formalised training process which begins to treat the beauty worker as a professional with recourse to formal qualifications and a code of professional standards and ethics. Despite these developments, the beauty and cosmetics industry did not become a fully recognisable, commercialised, mass industry until the 1920s and 1930s. Perhaps only after the Second World War does the industry with which we are familiar today actually consolidate itself.

In the past few years *The 1900 House* has been screened on British TV. In this programme a white middle-class family were returned to live in a house from the period of 1900. All fixtures, fittings, furnishings and facilities in the house were from this period. The family was allowed access only to products which would have been available to middle-class British families of the day. What was so striking was the way in which life for the woman was virtually unbearable in terms of the difficulties of her domestic duties, her personal surroundings and her social role – and this was a middle-class lifestyle. It is difficult to imagine how exhausting and miserable life would have been for poor women of the period. Also interesting was the fact that she had access to no pre-prepared beauty products. Washing her hair became a struggle with raw eggs and barely concealed disgust at having to live with greasy hair full of odours. Hands were constantly chapped from washing and other domestic chores, and the woman attempted to concoct her own hand cream from a mixture of glycerine and other ingredients. This preparation sufficed for face cream and was described as feeling similar to wax on the face. For the man of the house, however, visits to the barber supplemented his own clumsy attempts to shave with a cut-throat razor. What this programme clearly illustrates is that even to middle-class women at the turn of the century in the UK, beauty preparations were not readily available. It also illustrates that the preparations desired were related as much to cleanliness and health issues as they were to any notion of 'beauty'.

The development of the beauty industry sheds light upon political, social, economic and cultural processes. The fluctuations in women's employment may be traced through the history of the beauty therapist and her employment. Political battles over the bodies of women may be traced through the treatments offered. Cultural contestations around the representation of gender and race in advertising are exemplified in advertising for hair and beauty products. Gender politics is also reflected in the representations of the lifestyle of women in advertisements. The boundaries of racial identity are also worked out and fought over in both the representations and practices of the beauty industry. All of these themes are evident from the mid-nineteenth century and earlier, but their specific formulation may be clearly traced by examining the history of the beauty salon, and the beauty industry more widely. Most historical work which has been carried out focuses upon the USA. This means that this history includes treatments not generally found in the UK beauty salon. Hairdressing and beauty salons are not separated in this US history. In this way, the politics of hair is encapsulated within the history of the beauty shop. African-American and European American salons share a common trajectory, and also specificities. The following overview attempts to outline the history of the development of the beauty business with a focus on the USA, at the same time paying attention to the similarities and differences evident in terms of ethnicity.

The beauty industry pre-nineteenth century and onwards

Prior to the mid-nineteenth century women did not generally wear visible make-up. What they were avidly interested in, however, were recipes for creams and preparations which would improve their complexion and provide the smooth, white complexion which signified the genteel lady. Recipes for skin creams and complexion lighteners could often be traced to folk remedies, the ingredients for which had been used for centuries. These preparations were used in the sixteenth and seventeenth centuries as part of a generalised knowledge held by women concerning general housekeeping duties, the growth of herbs, treatment of the sick, and their own beauty routines. Preparations were used to combat the effects of illness such as smallpox or to reduce or promote colour in the complexion. In this sense the 'cosmetic' use of these preparations was clearly linked to a wider care of the body, and to general health care. The use of herbal and other preparations was also sometimes based upon an ideology of mysticism or astrology. Some of the preparations used also borrowed from a variety of cultures. In the USA, Mexican Americans brought with them traditional remedies such as using the 'warm urine of a small boy' as a cosmetic and a cure for skin disorders (Peiss, 1998). Slaves too brought with them hair and beauty preparations from West Africa. Native American use of roots and herbs also became known generally as 'Indian medicine'.

By the Victorian era these types of self-remedy were well known and women distributed recipes for a variety of skin treatments. It was also possible for women with access to some degree of disposable income to purchase beauty elixirs. The market began to expand partly due to the availability in drugstores and wholesalers of the ingredients for treatments, and many pre-prepared lotions. These types of outlet also developed a distribution network, expanding further the market for these products. What this early market focused on was urban women with access to disposable income, and to the ingredients or products desired. A small cosmetic industry developed and hair treatments were also popular. Similarly, perfumiers were important in this early development of the market. However, most sales focused around preparations for improving the complexion rather than the application of cosmetics.

The Victorians feared that cosmetics were a paint which could be used as a mask (Synnott, 1990). For centuries men had been suspicious of the use of such 'artifice', fearing that they could be trapped into marriage by the false appearance of the 'temptress' determined to lure them. Face paints could be used to disguise disfigurement from disease, or to rejuvenate the appearance of an older woman. Men saw the use of cosmetics as an unfair weapon in the armoury of unscrupulous women. However, a second reason for suspicion around the use of cosmetics was also evident. The use of make-up is associated with prostitution and with stage make-up used by actresses. In Victorian times and earlier, actresses themselves were viewed as little better than prostitutes in terms of their 'loose morals'. Make-up is thus associated with the whore side of the Madonna/whore dichotomy. The conspicuous display of cosmetic use among 'respectable' Victorian women could bring stares in public, and violent disapproval from men and women alike. The 'good' woman was reflected in her 'natural' appearance. However, this natural appearance was also highly regulated. The most popular preparations purchased by white Victorian women were skin lighteners. These were designed to give the pale, alabaster appearance so valued in middle-class Victorian society. This appearance of course was not always possible to achieve naturally, and middle-class women invested in skin lighteners and powders to present an appearance which signified a number of things.

First, pale skin signifies a lack of physical labour and exposure to the elements. Middle-class Victorian women signified upon their bodies that their lives were constrained by propriety, and clear class boundaries. Second, the use of powders designed to reduce perspiration and shine achieved a similar effect. This provided the illusion that women did not perspire, that they did not need to exert themselves, and as a result that they achieved some level of naturalised pale skin beauty.

Finally, and most importantly, the use of preparations to 'whiten' the appearance of the skin is a clear indicator of racial boundaries. Nineteenth-century commentators viewed beauty in relationship to race. Even the concept of 'race' itself was invented during this period and its usage remained unstable, sometimes referring to culture, sometimes to nature and sometimes to ethnic subgroups (McClintock, 1995). The solidification of the term to refer to the segmentation of various cultural groups into separate and distinct biologically based 'races' was a product of Victorian political rule and of imperialism which was supported by scientific arguments. This was especially true for Britain and its colonial Empire. Science was used to justify racial exploitation by the linkage of physical appearance with intellectual, moral and social characteristics. A racial hierarchy was constructed placing the white male Anglo-Saxon at the pinnacle. At the base of this hierarchy stood Africans, and those of African descent. In between lay a complex set of relationships between class, race and gender. Such a hierarchy supported the aspirations of white women to ensure and display their whiteness in order to secure privilege. The emphasis upon enhancing characteristics which supposedly signified the differences between the races was a preoccupation designed to deny the inter-connected history of white women with slavery, and with the fact that interracial relationships, and children as the product of those relationships, were common in both UK and US society. It is also clear that black women too made use of skin lighteners and bleaches. Although some commentators suggest that their use among specific groups of women should be seen more as parody than emulation (White and White, 1998, cited in Peiss, 1998), it seems that in a highly racialised society where privilege is linked to racial identity, it is no surprise that there should be a market among black women for products designed to modify appearance in line with characteristics which are correlated with that privilege.

Gilman (1999) also points out that what he calls 'aesthetic surgery' has long been used to alter racial characteristics, not only for black men and women but also for other minority groups.

What beauty preparations did for white middle-class Victorians then was to mark class and racial boundaries, as well as divisions within classes. They also established an image of delicate and natural femininity which Bhavani (1997) argues still operates today. She points out that this image of feminine beauty is built upon the domestic labour of white and black working-class women which allowed white middle-class women to live in this protected and privileged state. In colonial India this meant the presence of non-white maids and servants in the houses of white women. In the USA the same duties were performed by African-American women, and in the UK it was white working-class women who carried out the domestic tasks which allowed the development of the image of the white Victorian lady as delicate and highly feminised. Even so, consumption of skin lighteners and powders among this group of women clearly illustrates their insecurities, and the need to reinforce the supposed naturalness of this class and racial hierarchy through their own labour upon the body. From the mid-nineteenth century we have a clear link to the past in terms of home-made remedies used by women, but also the use of some preparations which are linked directly to the social and political climate of the day.

An important development during this period was the growth of an urban middle class which was attuned to the pleasures of display and consumption. This change coincided with some loosening of social hierarchies. At the same time an early feminist movement developed which led to fears that women demanding equality in the public sphere would lead to a loss of femininity among women in general. Seeing and being seen took on new meanings and importance in the late nineteenth-century city. Middle-class women partook of a new range of social engagements. The development of the department store allowed women to enter this public space as consumers, or simply as voyeurs. In fact Winship has suggested that women were drawn into this expanding consumer culture partly as an attempt to diffuse some of the demands of early feminism which was fuelled by the expansion of the numbers of women in paid employment, and by their demands for economic independence (Winship, 1987). Department stores were originally designed to be attractive to women, as women became the engines of the growth in consumption. For example, upon opening in London in 1909 Selfridges was the largest purpose-built store in the world, and the first department store to open in the UK. Through its innovative sales techniques it expanded the class spectrum of its customers and extended the potential for consumption to the middle classes. Selfridge himself was a supporter of women's suffrage, and also placed advertisements in the feminist press of the time (Nava, 1998). In fact, Mr Selfridge actually suggested that he was aiding the cause of women's emancipation through the opening of his store (Lury, 1997).

The introduction of street lighting into this increasingly visual urban culture altered the way people viewed themselves and others in public space. In earlier centuries and even at the beginning of the nineteenth century, the standard of glass was poor, and most people would have had only the vaguest notion of their own facial characteristics. At this time the quality of shop glass and looking glass improved, but the introduction of photography also had a huge impact on the way women and men viewed themselves. Victorian photography parlours could often look forward to repeat visits from clients who were not satisfied with their appearance. There was a high demand for pictures to be altered and tinted. Coinciding with these developments, the fashion and media industries also began to flourish. Women's magazines carried advertisements for skin creams, yet continued to publish only limited information or advertising for cosmetics. The debate around whether women should 'paint' retained its force until the First World War. This phase from the mid-nineteenth century into the twentieth is neatly summarised by Peiss as coinciding with the growth in consumerism and commercialisation:

> Women's growing interest in beauty products coincided with their new sense of identity as consumers. Women had long bought and bartered goods, but around 1900 a new, self-

> conscious notion of the woman consumer emerged. Women's magazines and advertisers inducted their female readers into a world of brand-name products and smart shopping, while department stores created a feminine paradise of abundance, pleasure and service.
>
> (Peiss, 1998, p. 50)

This identity as consumer, although widespread, could not yet be regarded as a mass market. For example, as late as 1916 it was estimated that only one in five Americans used toilet preparations of any sort (ibid.). It is here that we need to think back to the British woman in her middle-class 1900 home, washing her hair in eggs and boiling up her own hand cream.

It was from this period onward that the beauty salon as we understand it began to develop. Prior to this date some salons had existed for very wealthy women, or women had used treatments at home. From the end of the nineteenth century, women entrepreneurs became involved in the manufacturing and marketing of beauty products, as well as in the setting up of beauty businesses. As Peiss comments, it is easy to view the contemporary multinational conglomerate structure of much of the beauty business as the norm. However, the roots of the industry are very different:

> Cosmetics today seem quintessentially products of a consumer culture dominated by large corporations, national advertising, and widely circulated images of ideal beauty. The origins of American beauty culture lie elsewhere, however, in a spider's web of businesses – beauty parlours, druggists, department stores, patent cosmetic companies, perfumers, mail-order houses, and women's magazines that thrived at the turn of the century and formed the nascent infrastructure of the beauty industry.
>
> (Peiss, 1998, p. 61)

It is also worth noting that even today, the delivery of treatment and sales relies on local networks. Certainly for the women in this study visits to the beauty salon are as much about experiences at a local level as they are about achieving a distant and universalised aesthetic ideal.

The turn of the century and into the twentieth

The forerunners of the beauty therapists in this study may be found in abundance in the turn-of-the-century beauty industry. The beauty business provided one of the few sources of employment open to women where their expertise propelled them to the highest levels of authority and entrepreneurship. At the end of the nineteenth century both working-class and some middle-class women entered the beauty business. Hairdressing and beauty salons often relied upon the women working within them to mix up their own preparations for use on the hair and bodies of clients. From the turn of the century women began to patent these formulas, and to manufacture and distribute them more commercially. Although many enterprises continued to consist of one woman in her kitchen, producing goods to distribute locally, there also stand out a number of businesswomen who developed national networks, large production capabilities, and who invested in advertising. Florence Nightingale Graham (later to become Elizabeth Arden) and Helena Rubenstein remain well-known names in the cosmetic industry. Annie Turnbow and Sarah Breedlove (Madam C. J. Walker) presided over similar business empires focused upon the African-American market. For these women, distribution was often a problem, and so they pioneered systems of home selling and mail order, copied by other businesses in later years. The vastly expanded numbers of women employed in the industry were also encouraged to learn the systems of care preferred by each of the beauty businesses. From the end of the nineteenth century formal training was established in hair and beauty courses. These were followed either through correspondence courses or in newly founded beauty schools. Again these enterprises were established and staffed by women. These newly trained women worked in the increasing number of beauty salons franchised to a particular system.

The women in this business, however, still faced the problem of establishing the 'respectability' of beauty as a business. Cosmetic use and 'beautifying' in general could still be scorned and associated with 'loose' morality, and vanity. Beauty routines were sold as a duty to women in order to preserve their own natural assets. They were also conspicuously marketed through the shared knowledge and tribulations of the female entrepreneurs themselves. In so doing they diminished earlier suspicion of cosmetics by:

> Promoting beauty care as a set of practices at once physical, individual, social and commercial. Their businesses transformed the personal *cultivation* of beauty – the original meaning of the expression 'beauty culture' – into a *culture* of shared meanings and rituals.
>
> (Peiss, 1998, p. 62)

This was achieved in no small part through the world of the beauty salon and local networks of women. Advertisements were most often placed in the local press, and word of mouth was used to spread news of a new product or treatment. The beauty salon acted as a homosocial world, one of the few semi-public spaces where women could meet openly. The market aimed at white women fragmented along income lines, with Helena Rubenstein, for example, aiming marketing campaigns at 'high society' women.

For African-American women, the market developed differently. Here, the salon was the centre of community and sometimes of political impulses. White-owned companies which had marketed to the black population, and black male-owned companies had sold skin lighteners and bleaches to women. The black women who owned beauty businesses took a different path, with key players in the industry refusing to market such products. Beauty businesses also acted as vital sources of employment for black women, and men. For example, the huge migration of black workers from the Southern USA to the North in the first part of the nineteenth century stimulated the need for vastly increased employment opportunities in Northern cities. Many black women worked as domestic labourers in the homes of the white population. However, one important source of self-employment was to enter the beauty business. As employment for barbers with a predominantly white male clientele decreased due to the worsening race relations during the great migration, African-American women expanded their own employment opportunities in serving their black female clientele (Boyd, 1996). In fact, as Boyd also points out, the famous Madam C. J. Walker was the first woman in the USA to become a self-made millionaire (Boyd, 1996, p. 42).

The beauty culture of black women was much more embedded into everyday culture. Salons and treatments received at home certainly brought together women in order to receive beauty treatments, and also to make money for the woman providing the services, but importantly these gatherings were the source of economic support later on, for example, during the depression, and the locations where politics could be discussed. In this sense beauty culture was tied to a wider ethical and political culture. The link between politics and Madam C. J. Walker's beauty business is clear. She was a supporter of the National Association for the Advancement of Coloured People, and campaigned against lynching. Her daughter Leila (who became A'leila) Walker later used the money inherited from her mother to become a patron of Harlem writers such as Zora Neale Hurston and Langston Hughes, and to found a night-club in Harlem (Rowbotham, 1997, p. 652). Both Walker and Annie Turnbow Malone contributed to community arts programmes, to training in black communities, and to fostering business ventures along family and ethical lines. Malone also addressed the women involved in her enterprises about politics.

In the first twenty years of the twentieth century the beauty industry developed and expanded. Between 1909 and 1929 in the USA the number of cosmetic and perfume manufacturers nearly doubled. During the same period the value of the market rose from $14.2 million to $141 million (Peiss, 1998, p. 97). A local service-orientated industry was built by women entrepreneurs. However, as the market for beauty products exploded, the industry was gradually taken over by men. In the USA, the food and drug act of 1906 had restricted the production and use of many of the ingredients in preparations made in the small-scale operations and salons. The establishment of professional organisations and the striving for a new professional respectability within the industry was initiated by the men newly associated with the beauty business, and had the effect of marginalising the small salon and the small-scale businesswoman (Willett, 2000). Older companies began to join with a new generation of male entrepreneurs to capitalise upon the expanded beauty market. Make-up still remained a riskier and more controversial product. However, companies that did enter this market vastly expanded the ranges women could choose from, even as the factories which manufactured the basic preparations remained small in number. A further development initiated in this newly male-dominated industry was to invest in advertising. Advertising in national magazines was particularly innovative and effective, although products were marketed to varied consumer niches. Beauty pages in women's magazines also became a feature. In this changing climate, the localism and specialised knowledge of women beauty entrepreneurs proved a disadvantage, and they became increasingly marginalised.

Although there were some parallels in the expansion of the market and developments within it, black-owned businesses were more immune to this trend as their markets and businesses were highly segmented. Black businesses served a black clientele and even advertised in a separate black press. White-owned businesses began to try to tap into this market either by marketing to black consumers, or by developing brands specifically for that market. This met with some resistance from black businesspeople and consumers alike. However, more established black-owned businesses did have to alter their methods and their products, although Madam C. J. Walker maintained her refusal to sell skin-lightening products. During the Great Depression of the 1930s, many small businesses closed, although the beauty salons also served as sources of economic and social support during the period. One feature which white and black segments of the market shared, however, was the increasing presence of men in the industry:

The consumer culture that emerged in the 1920s, with its emphasis on advertising and media based marketing, is today so integral to American life that it appears an inevitable, almost natural development. Cosmetics, consumption, and femininity seem part of a seamless fabric. In this formative period, however, mass-market firms actively searched for ways to package their goods that would legitimize cosmetic products and practices still questionable in the eyes of many Americans. Gaining insight into women consumers, and channelling their apparent needs and desires into sales, remained a perplexing problem for many of the men who now ran the cosmetics industry.

(Peiss, 1998, p. 114)

White businessmen in the beauty market were keen to distance themselves from any hint of effeminacy, and often presented themselves as men with a scientific background, or with knowledge of the theatrical world. These male-owned companies would hire a well-known and 'glamorous' woman to endorse their products. Sometimes they created the illusion of a female-owned company. In addition, such companies sought the knowledge and expertise of women in marketing and advertising. A significant group of well-educated women became taste formers and cultural intermediaries in the process of accommodating women's fashion and style with the business needs of the beauty industry. The women in these positions experienced a contradiction which forms a precedent for some of the workplace ambiguities I discuss in Chapter 4. Although intelligent and professional women, their expertise was viewed as somehow 'natural'. It was implied that their success in fields such as advertising rested upon this female empathy rather than on professional skills and qualifications. This echoes the difficulties experienced by beauty therapists in my own study who emphasised empathy and listening skills as vital to their professional role. At the same time these are precisely the types of skills which women are seen to possess by virtue of their femininity rather than by training (Sharma and Black, 2001).

Increasingly, synergies developed between businesses such as advertisers, retailers, manufacturers and magazine editors. One cultural form which played a particularly important role in promoting the use of cosmetics and beauty products was the cinema (Stacey, 1994). The cinema had already done much to popularise a made-up look, and this was used in the direct marketing of products. What cinema also did was to promote femininity as a process of image selection. It offered a set of ready-made types which could be selected from and purchased along with the beauty and fashion products represented in popular films (Craik, 1994).

One of the key shifts here is noticeable in the linkage of fashion and clothing to cosmetics. In the nineteenth century beauty products were sold as enhancing natural beauty, and as what we would today recognise as general grooming. Make-up use itself was considered daring. From the 1920s onward appearance is linked to fashion, and the look of the face itself becomes subject to style (Craik, 1994). For example, in the USA in 1937, the leading cosmetics trade journal changed its name from *Toilet Requisites* to *Beauty Fashion* (Peiss, 1998, p. 130). By the beginning of the Second World War the beauty industry had been increasingly commodified, and had become a mass market. Women entrepreneurs and workers in the industry had been sidelined, and the business of beauty became linked to fashion rather than to any idea of a transhistorical grooming or enhancement process. Culture had become increasingly visualised, and magazines and the cinema became major sources of fashion images and advice for women. This then became the beauty industry as we recognise it in its present form.

During the Second World War, femininity and its signifiers were co-opted into the political service of the war effort. Women were drafted in to work in occupations dominated previously by men. Women worked in armaments factories, operated heavy machinery and drove large vehicles. They engaged in heavy manual labour, all in the name of the war effort. Although it should be noted that working-class women had always worked in heavy industry, the jobs they performed were segregated from those of men, and so although some women were used to factory work and manual labour, they were not experienced in all aspects of this work. The professions also saw an influx of women during this period. In the UK, middle-class women in these types of occupations were more likely to want to remain in their employment at the end of the war, while women in poorly paid and monotonous factory work looked forward to a return to their pre-war lives (Rowbotham, 1997).

The arrival of women in these new sites of labour was not always welcomed by the male employees. There are incidences of male employees in the UK sabotaging machinery to be used by women. Skilled working men also feared that women would undermine their trade union rights (Rowbotham, 1997). At the base of these fears though was gender and class politics. Appeals to femininity by the women themselves, and by advertisers attempted to diffuse some of this unease around the role of women. In the UK, women took to dyeing their legs in the absence of stockings, often appealing to friends to draw a straight line up the backs of their legs, thus giving the impression of a stocking seam. In the USA an advertisement by Tangee, a cosmetic company, appeared in women's magazines in 1943 and 1944. The ad encouraged the use of lipstick, even though the world was at war, and congratulated women on 'keeping your femininity – even though you are doing a man's work' (quoted in Peiss, 1998, p. 240). Lipstick became a powerful symbol of femininity and was used to boost morale and increase productivity. In 1942, cosmetic manufacture in the USA was limited, and new products were banned from the market in an attempt to conserve essential materials. However, four months later the limitation order was repealed. Cosmetic use had come to be seen as essential to the war effort in terms of the role it played in securing women's commitment. As Peiss states, 'Beautifying had evolved from an everyday grooming habit into an assertion of American national identity' (Peiss, 1998, p. 245). However, the use of cosmetics was carefully managed, with a too overtly feminised appearance in factories being frowned upon. Clothes, hair-styles and make-up became areas of concern around safety in the work environment, but also sources of anxiety about femininity and the appropriate role of women during a period of social change. This new linkage of appearance, cosmetics, fashion and identity then is a theme which runs throughout the development of the beauty industry from the Second World War to the present day.

Post-war

By the end of the war cosmetic use had become part of a culture of femininity, no longer either seen as suspicious for its potential to mask the true women underneath, and also in general disassociated from prostitution and 'loose morals'. By 1948 in the USA, almost 90 per cent of adult women used lipstick (Peiss, 1998, p. 245). However, markets were segmented along class, geographical and ethnic lines. It is during this period that the science of demographics becomes linked to lifestyle, advertising and the beauty industry. It is also during the 1950s that the meaning of cosmetic and beauty product use is removed from the sphere of performance and linked instead to the idea of a natural femininity. Paradoxically, then, cosmetic use and beauty preparations are sold to women as bringing out their real inner beauty, or as enhancing their true nature. Artificiality is sold under the guise of a natural, already present femininity. This was accompanied by, for example, the development of cosmetics which clung to the skin, so that foundation or lipstick which did not rub off played upon its qualities of indelibility.

The lives of middle-class women in the 1950s and early 1960s imprisoned in suburban homes is well documented. Writers such as Betty Friedan (1963) and Hannah Gavron (1966) captured the frustration, repression and boredom of the times. For Friedan this was the 'problem that has no name':

> The problem lay buried, unspoken, for many years in the minds of American women. It was a strange stirring, a sense of dissatisfaction, a yearning that women suffered in the middle of the twentieth century in the United States. Each suburban wife struggled with it alone. As she made the beds, shopped for groceries, matched slipcover material, ate peanut butter sandwiches with her children, chauffeured Cub Scouts

and Brownies, lay beside her husband at night, she was afraid to ask even of herself the silent question: 'Is this all'?

(Friedan, 1963, p. 13)

In Marianne Faithful's 'Ballad of Lucy Jordan' the only escape from this 'white suburban bedroom in a white suburban home' is suicide (Marianne Faithful, 1979). However, as feminist writers were suggesting liberation as the solution, cosmetic companies were selling the ideals of fantasy and escapism to these Lucy Jordans of their day. Sexuality too became part of this escapism, and advertisements begin to engage with female sexuality as a marketing tool.

The emergence of the teenage market during this period was both a function of the increasing sophistication of advertisers to segment and develop particular markets, and also of a changing social context. As make-up use had become subject increasingly to psychological interpretation during the 1950s, so too did cosmetic use become linked to questions of identity. Young women in the 1950s saw experimenting with appearance as a vital element to their own developing sense of femininity. It was also part of social rituals enmeshed in the culture of young women. Trying on clothes, experimenting with hairstyles and the application of make-up forms a large and important part of the friendship rituals of young women. The use of make-up from the 1950s also came increasingly to signify a rite of passage which denoted entry into 'womanhood'. From the 1960s young women were using appearance to mark distinctions between themselves and an older generation, but also between different cliques within youth culture. Advertising and cosmetic companies were keen to market their products to these segmented markets, and designed products which would appeal to a variety of different social and cultural groups.

The demands of the army during the Second World War ensured that men had learned how to appear neat and tidy, to pay attention to personal hygiene, and to ensure their hair was well presented. During this period male grooming products were marketed vigorously, and male toiletries were presented as morale boosters in the way that women's cosmetics had been. This market was capitalised upon after the war and advertising was developed which targeted different groups of men. Appearance became important in the competitive corporate business world. In addition, younger men embraced grooming products. The two most common images to appear were those of the military hero and the romantic man. In order to avoid any hint of homosexuality or femininity in their campaigns, advertisers pushed the 'romantic' male image into scenes of sexual aggressiveness (Peiss, 1998).

For African-Americans, appearance continued to be important after the war. Expenditure on personal care products rose steadily, and black-owned businesses continued to cater to this growing clientele. Exclusion from the white mainstream press was one source of disquiet, with black models being absent from women's and beauty magazines. By the late 1950s and 1960s political activism was linked to beauty culture by black Americans. A growing civil rights movement politicised appearance, and the use of hair straighteners and skin lighteners declined. The 'Afro' was adopted as a fashion and a political statement, and the phrase 'Black is Beautiful' was used in order to elevate the markers of race to a position of pride. However, the ambivalence of this position was expressed by Gil Scott-Heron in 'Brother', where he discusses how a young male black revolutionary encourages a black woman to stop straightening her hair and to grow an Afro. As Scott-Heron points out, however, the young black man will not speak to this same woman if, as a result of her actions, she 'looks like hell' (Scott-Heron, 1989 [1970]). The Nation of Islam too adopted a potentially contradictory position in standing against hair straightening yet at the same time supporting black-owned business, a significant proportion of which were beauty salons where hair straightening was a core source of income (Craig, 2002). A critique of the hegemony of white beauty was also linked to a critique of capitalism, and the beauty industry was seen as a financial exploiter of black women. Ironically perhaps, beauty salons catering to an African-American clientele formed one of the community locations where information about the civil rights movement was passed on, and from where political resistance was supported and organised. Craig (2002) also points out that within the civil rights movement there was disagreement about the role of beauty contests, with some activists arguing that they exploited women, and others that contests for black women promoted racial pride and ideals of success. The disagreements here were as much about gender politics as they were about race.

It is during the 1960s and 1970s that the fashion and beauty industry begins to receive political critique. Prior to this date, although we sometimes see resistance to the use of cosmetics, and criticism on moral grounds, the area of 'beauty' had not been viewed as a legitimate political concern. The black civil rights movement introduced politics into this arena and this was quickly taken up by feminists. The phrase 'the personal is political' is an echo of the way that appearance could no longer be seen simply as an individual, or unimportant issue. The modification and commodification of women's bodies had become both a personal, a public and a political issue. Fashion styles fractured. Among the 1960s counter-culture, the 'natural body' was promoted. Unmade-up women, body hair, and long hair for both women and men were considered erotic, and also somehow authentic and 'real'. However, this type of look was also adopted by those who did not adhere to these theoretical underpinnings, and simply adopted the style as a fashion.

Black politics and counter-cultural politics also formed part of the inspiration for feminist critiques of the beauty industry. Beauty contests became a target for political activism. The beauty industry was criticised more widely, and the role of advertising in particular was brought under scrutiny. The beauty industry was linked to wider questions of patriarchal oppression and racism. Patriarchal capitalism was seen as promoting the unattainable and 'un-natural' ideal for women to aspire to (Chapkis, 1986). This had the effect not only of drawing women into a system of commodification and consumption, but also of turning them into objects of the 'male gaze'.

While these critiques may have been successful in intellectual and political terms, the cosmetic industry was not necessarily weakened by them. It responded by repackaging its products. For example, the *Clinique* range was launched not as a beauty product but as a scientifically endorsed method of maintaining cleanliness and grooming. By using asexual imagery, pared down packaging, and white-coated advisers in retail outlets, *Clinique* deliberately focused on the professional market. The 'liberated woman' became an advertising type, and the rejection of make-up among feminists was reinterpreted in the industry as the 'natural look'. From this point onward it has not been possible to understand the beauty industry without reference to politics. As Peiss states:

> The debate over cosmetics today veers noisily between the poles of victimization and self-invention, between the prison of beauty and the play of make-up.
>
> (Peiss, 1998, p. 269)

The discourse of choice has entered the arguments not only of consumers but has also been a powerful tool used by the beauty industry itself. This question of choice and identity is explored further in the following chapter.

Chapter 3

Just because it feels good doesn't make it right

Identity in the beauty salon

> Feminist theory on beauty needs to be grounded; that is, it must take the ambiguous, contradictory, everyday social practices of women as its starting point.
>
> (Davis, 1991, p. 33)

I have chosen the beauty salon as a site *par excellence*, where attainment of femininity and its definition are being negotiated. In its generally closed and intimate nature, the beauty salon is not only a feminised space, but also one in which the secret routines of femininity are commodified and exemplified. Much feminist writing has been concerned to criticise the operation of the beauty industry, but has generally remained ungrounded in empirical settings. It has also remained critical of some practices while neglecting others. Those practices which relate to appearance have come in for particular criticism. In approaching this complex area I agree broadly with Davis' statement above. What might a grounded theorisation of the beauty salon look like? How might the feminist critique of the beauty industry be refined if the salon was placed in historical perspective, and if the testimonies of clients and therapists themselves were taken into account?

The women in this study were in no sense unambiguously oppressed in their use of the salon. A complex web of social, cultural, economic and political factors contribute to the reasons why women choose to visit beauty salons. None of the clients remained unambiguous in their use. They were all self-critical to some extent. They were also critical of the commodified system into which they were buying:

> What they [beauty industry] are selling is just a mask. It's not really the nuts and bolts of people is it? It's just a kind of image that you can buy or not buy.
>
> (Madeleine)

Some mentioned feminism and the belief that they should not be concerned with appearance. Others believed that salons were not for 'people like them', so justifying their treatments as an unavoidable necessity. Still others regarded their time spent in salons as a luxury, or a treat which had to be earned. Such pampering was earned through working hard, or through devoting time and energy to family and the demands of others. There is no simplistic or unidirectional model to be constructed here which will explain the effects of the beauty industry upon unsuspecting 'cultural dopes'. Similarly, there is no absolute freedom to play with signification practices and bodies either. In this way, although I begin with the everyday social practices of women themselves, these may be understood only within the context of constrained potentialities.

In trying to make sense of the interviews with beauty salon clients, I have been struck by the internal logic to their stories and their claims. Within each narrative, the treatments chosen, the priorities assessed and the other treatments rejected as mere 'luxuries' make perfect sense. It was logical for Anna who worked on the door of a night-club to have her nails painted and extended. The fact of their visibility reinforced her femininity in a male-dominated job, a world of masculine heterosexual display. It was both emotional and convincing to listen to Patricia who claimed that she would rather not eat in order to afford the electrolysis which reduced facial hair, than to suffer the agony of self-consciously living with that hair. Woven into the account of each salon visit lies an internal consistency. However, I have been unable to predict what types of treatment a woman will prefer, or what will be her one 'thing', that which she describes as a necessity or a preference. This world of preferences and priorities is complex and confusing. When reading an individual narrative, all becomes clear, but when stepping back to include all the women interviewed, the picture becomes a kaleidoscope of class, gender, age, income, ethnicity and so on. However, as with the kaleidoscope, patterns can be identified, and much of the time these regularities form familiar patterns. In order to understand this kaleidoscopic view I refer to the position occupied by the woman. For Bourdieu (1998), action is both relational and dispositional; that is, it is made up of objective relations which cannot be shown but which must be captured and inferred, and of potentialities which are inscribed in the bodies of agents. The cornerstone of this philosophy is the two-way relationship between objective structures (social fields) and incorporated structures (habitus) (Bourdieu, 1998). I am drawing on this framework in understanding the situatedness of the woman in wider social relations. This position is the objective location in relation to structural factors. I regard these structural factors as including class, ethnicity, sexuality and gender. My use of position could also be understood as subjectivity. In contrast, I also refer to biography, which is the particular configuration of these objective social conditions in the life of the particular woman. This could also be described as her identity (Stacey, 1997). I do not intend my use of identity or biography to be understood in any individualised sense. Rather, the configurations of class, age, ethnicity, gender and sexuality position the woman in a web of relationships and potentialities, but a web within which she is able to exercise these potentialities within a particular biographical location. It is important to understand this complex and constraining context, as writers on the beauty industry too often leave women's behaviour to an undertheorised concept of 'socialisation' or the equally simplistic 'internalisation' of feminine ideals. In this chapter I will grapple with these complex explanations while attempting to ground theoretical explanations with empirical data.

Below I outline the two areas into which I have broken down women's relationship with the beauty salon: getting in; and getting it right. Although these broad headings are my own classifications, the subheadings contained within each are based on grounded empirical concepts. What I believe we see operating is the habitus, but the habitus exhibited in a specifically gendered form, relating as it does here to the highly feminised world of the beauty salon. Getting in and getting it right may be seen as empirically based heuristic devices for examining the operation of the habitus in relation to the social position of the women in this study, and by extrapolation, to women more widely.

Getting in relates to the processes women are engaged in before they actually visit the beauty salon. What compels a woman to make her first visit? In what context does a visit to the beauty salon begin to seem like a legitimate, and sometimes necessary, act? Getting it right relates to the 'doing' of femininity but also to the achievement of what I have termed an 'appropriate' state of being and looking. This achievement of appropriate femininity is cross-cut by other sociological categories. It is in this 'getting it right' that we see most clearly their operation, and the relevance of feminist critiques. The services consumed by clients may be related back to their decision to purchase the services of the beauty salon – how the woman first gets through the door. The types of treatments accessed require the client to draw on different justificatory discourses. The labour involved in 'getting it right' also influences which services the client believes are necessary for her (pampering; health; routine grooming; corrective). In later chapters I outline in more depth how specific practices may be related closely to the woman's own social position in the wider world outside. In particular, I focus on the arenas of work and health to illustrate how the treatments received by the client are implicated in her fulfilment of social demands in the wider social context.

Getting in

First, I will analyse the process whereby salon visits are initiated. The overarching framework within which beauty salon visits are experienced is that of a negotiation between what I have called self-view, worldview and appropriateness. Self-view and world-view may be seen broadly as two aspects of what Bourdieu has described as 'the habitus' (Bourdieu, 1990; Crossley, 2001). I feel it is useful here to make a distinction between how the woman views her own actions and how she places these in terms of a wider worldview. In this sense, self-view is inward looking and world-view is outward looking. However, both are part of an internalised framework based on social position. It is this social position which will influence how she 'does' gender, and this is what I am referring to in using the concept of appropriateness.

Self-view

Self-view relates to the person that the client sees herself as. Am I the kind of person who visits salons? Am I the kind of woman who spends money on herself? Am I the kind of woman who spends money on cosmetic products and beauty treatments? All women in the study felt that they had to justify their association with the beauty salon. This justificatory process highlights the lengths women go to to avoid the more negative connotations of beauty salon use. Being associated with looks and beauty carries with it the potential for accusations of vanity. It also carries negative moral associations of laziness and self-obsession. In addition, as both Bartky (1997) and Wolf (1990) point out, for women to overtly spend time on such 'trivialities' devalues their own status and claims to skills and knowledge:

> To succeed in the provision of a beautiful or sexy body gains a woman attention and some admiration but little real respect and rarely any social power. A woman's effort to master feminine bodily discipline will lack importance just because she does it.
>
> (Bartky, 1997, p. 73)

The beauty/brains dichotomy is one which haunts beauty therapists. In their association with the beauty side of the split through their employment it is difficult to simultaneously claim knowledge and skills associated with the 'brains' side. For other women also, too close an association with the body and appearance reinforces a relationship to femininity which is not a positive status to acquire. Femininity and masculinity are correlated with the mind/body duality (Grosz, 1994, p. 4). To be associated with the body is to be more closely associated with nature, with femininity, and to lie at odds with rational thought and the elevated work of the mind. This tension is experienced as a bifurcated consciousness; although both the client and the therapist realise that the attainment of appropriate femininity is necessary, they are also left without the language or conceptual framework to articulate this work in anything other than derogatory terms (Smith, 1987). Although not spoken about in precisely this way, women are well aware of the risks of these associations. Many of the clients interviewed, therefore, did not claim to be the type of women who visited salons (and therefore to be preoccupied with the body). In each case they provided their own justification for their visits in terms which relate to the four-part schema I have outlined above. It is also for this reason that none of the women in the salon associate their visits with beauty; rather they provide explanations for their treatment choices in terms of reference to their own biographical specificities, and also in wider sociological terms. In order to overcome these negative associations, the therapists emphasise the 'therapy' side to their work and downplay the 'beauty' aspect of their title:

> I would say that it does offer a very high therapeutic angle to it, it boosts people's confidence and self-esteem. Some people, I think, misinterpret what vanity is. If somebody said years ago 'I am going to a beauty therapist's', you instantly thought beauty and vanity, the two go together. But these days there's more to salons, there's more emphasis on stress-related problems and that, massage is good to release stress and these other therapies have come forward, reflexology, aromatherapy, shiatsu.

> (Kerry BT)

Linked to this disavowal is the traditional image that the public more generally are believed to hold of beauty salons and their clients. 'Ladies who lunch' was a phrase which recurred to describe what women had thought of beauty salon clients before they themselves began to visit for treatments. This carries with it connotations of a specific social class location, of a white racial identity, of significant amounts of disposable income and of leisure. It also implies an over-reliance upon appearance and the trappings of femininity. This combination of economic position, available leisure time and adherence to ideals of femininity implies a specific middle-class location which is at odds with the middle-class career woman more often to be found in the beauty salons I studied. The expansion of the beauty sector and the increase in the types of treatments available has brought into relief this distinction within middle-class identity. While previously salon attendance might have been associated with leisured upper-middle-class women, today the beauty salon is more likely to be populated by employed middle-class and working-class women who are keen to disassociate themselves from the 'ladies who lunch'.

Beauty salons also project an image of feminine perfection to those who have not entered their doors. Clients describe their fear of finding model-like women with 'legs up to their armpits' populating the salon. They expect to find women who have achieved some idealised notion of femininity both staffing and visiting the salon. They spoke of their relief upon visiting salons to discover that both clients and staff were in fact 'ordinary'. Therapists themselves acknowledge that this is the image held by the public at large and they see this as unjustified, and also as one factor which prevents women from making initial visits. They also explain this as one of the reasons why clients often prefer older therapists, described here by Yvette as 'past it':

> Not everyone wants to walk into a salon and see a blonde 'bimbo' you know, with legs up to her armpits to make them feel intimidated. I mean people are ordinary. Ordinary people come through here. Elderly people come through here and they're pleased to see me because I'm past it [laughs].
>
> (Yvette BT)

This exclusionary image of the salon is modified in other studies which identify how local salons can be seen as a social meeting place. For example, in her study of a salon, Furman identifies how both ethnicity and age are key in drawing women into the 'emotional climate of women's friendship, support, and camaraderie' (Furman, 1997, p. 1). This situation is most likely in the USA and other countries where the salon is an open and communal space, and where the introduction to the salon is made by others who share the same social group. This is also more likely to be the case where the salon is locally owned, rather than part of a large conglomerate.

Self-view thus relates to the image that the client holds of salons and her relationship to this image which is displayed through the consumption of leisure practices:

> Leisure has been invented as the domain of free choice par excellence. However constrained by external or internal factors, the modern self is institutionally required to construct a life through the exercise of choice from among alternatives. Every aspect of life, like every commodity, is imbued with a self-referential meaning; every choice we make is an emblem of our identity, a mark of our individuality, each is a message to ourselves and others as to the sort of person we are, each casts a glow back, illuminating the self of he or she who consumes.
>
> (Rose, 1999, p. 231)

In describing 'what type of person I am', women are constantly creating a distinction between themselves and other people. In consuming practices, services and products which fit with this view they are creating distinctions which serve the important function of creating the self. By avoiding associations with women who are concerned only with appearance they associate themselves with characteristics which carry if not positive connotations, then at least avoid the more negative associations of feminine tastes and consumption practices (Sparke, 1995).

Specific language is also used in order to draw distinctions between herself and the symbolic 'ladies who lunch'. Salons have done much work to counteract this image, for example, by emphasising the 'ordinary' nature of their clients and staff, or by offering treatments which contribute to the 'well-being' of the client rather than simply to alterations in her appearance. Here the salon owner must know her clientele and market the salon accordingly if it is to support the self-view of the potential customer. The situation of the salon in terms of ownership, location, treatments offered and the arrangement of internal space is crucial in appealing to a segmented market. The expansion of treatments marketed as contributing to the well-being of the client has been buoyed by the trend towards increasing use of complementary therapies. Partly as a result of the iatrogenic effects of conventional biomedicine, and also due partly to the increasing awareness of alternative views of health linked to lifestyle positions, complementary therapies such as massage, reiki, aromatherapy, shiatsu and others have become more widely available and popular (Cant and Sharma, 1995). The beauty salon has picked up on this expanding market and, according to its selected clientele, has been able to reposition itself to appeal to these potential clients. In addition, the increasing commodification of the body has widened the number of services targeted at the body (Featherstone, 1982). The beauty salon client, therefore, can now more easily justify her salon use in leisure, consumption or health terms and avoid the negative connotations of vanity.

Worldview

Worldview, although related to self-view, forms a set of beliefs or philosophy which informs the self-view, and allows a woman to place her actions within a wider moral framework. Worldview might relate to the belief that it is or is not appropriate to spend disposable income on beauty products and services. For example, Lisa claimed that because of her work in hospitals she was able to view poverty and ill-health which had not formed a part of her economically comfortable upbringing. This experience had radically altered her personal philosophy and led her to criticise the women she knew before moving to university who would spend considerable amounts of income on manicures and other 'non-essential' beauty treatments. Madeleine related her experience of working in the fashion industry and being able to view the poor working conditions and low wages of those whose job it was to sew designer clothes. As a result of this early formative experience she had changed career and was reluctant to buy into a wider fashion/beauty industry:

> I found these illegal immigrants working in a very small place with mould growing up the walls and the condensation was so bad that actually some of the machines were sitting in pools of water. I am not exaggerating, this is what I actually found. And this is a bit disgusting, and do excuse me, but the final thing was going to another unit and that was in the basement and even worse . . . and of course nobody had any say because they were illegal immigrants, but I went to this place where the women didn't even have proper sanitary provision. They just had to put the towels or whatever they had used into a cloth or box in the toilet and it was just absolutely disgusting. And I just said to them [employer] 'I will not work in an industry where you have got people doing things like that'.
>
> (Madeleine)

Madeleine justified her trips to the salon and purchase of products by shopping at the *Body Shop*, a chain of stores and salons marketed on the basis of a fair trade policy with suppliers of raw materials farmed in the developing world, and a commitment to ecological issues. She explained that their policies meant that she could shop there without guilt, and also reinforce her own worldview in the process. In a few cases worldview also included mention of feminism and the belief that women should neither spend much of their time concerned with personal appearance, nor be judged upon it:

I suppose it's all part of the beauty industry thing. Ten years
ago I wouldn't have considered doing it for feminist
reasons. . . . It's like something else that I have done that I
kind of didn't do for a long time was to lose weight, and it's
like that in a way. I always knew that I would be pressured
by society to lose weight, and I was the shape I was, but nevertheless two or three years ago I thought, 'I'll lose weight and
see what it is like', and I did. But it's the same kind of dichotomy, is that the right word? On the one side I know I
shouldn't be pressurised into that and I know it's the fault of
society and all that kind of thing, but on the other hand I do
it anyway.

(Laura)

All the interviewees then worked to reconcile their own self-view
and worldview with their visits to the salon. In order to do so they
described their own treatments in a manner which avoided contradiction with this philosophical framework. I have described the
four categories of treatments which women access in salons: regular
grooming; health treatments; pampering; and corrective treatments. The differences between these types of treatments enable
the client to align her salon use with her self-view and worldview.
However, ambivalence was a constant presence in the narratives
and in the experiences of the women. While they were able to
question the nature and value of the beauty industry, and even to
reject certain elements of it, the very fact of their presence in the
salon meant that they had been unable to reject it wholesale. This
ambivalence seems to suggest that writers such as Chapkis (1986),
who argue for a strategic disengagement with the beauty industry
as a means of affecting political change, have underestimated the
power that the achievement of a femininity grounded in physicality
holds for women. Why did the women tolerate this ambivalence?
One suggestion offered by Bartky (1990) is that to disavow the
external symbols of femininity equates to an annihilation of the self:

To have a body felt to be 'feminine' – a body socially constructed through the appropriate practices – is in most cases

crucial to a woman's sense of herself as female and, since persons currently can only be as male and female, to her sense of herself as an existing individual. To possess such a body may also be essential to her sense of herself as a sexually desiring and desirable subject. Hence, any political project that aims to dismantle the machinery that turns a female body into a feminine one may well be apprehended by a woman as something that threatens her with desexualisation, if not outright annihilation.

(Bartky, 1990, p. 105)

Ambivalence then is understandable. Women may recognise the deeply oppressive and reactionary forces at work within the beauty industry, yet at the same time are unable to fully reject engagement with such practices without risk to their very sense of being. In this sense women are identified as feminine and placed as such rather than having the freedom to self-identify, or even to reject, such an identity (Butler, 1993; Bourdieu, 2001). The position of women is hegemonically defined as biological, while at the same time requiring investment in 'artifice' to maintain this veneer of naturalness. However, given this level of constraint, it should also be noted that most of the treatments received in the salon are physically pleasurable and this sensuousness plays an important role in preventing disengagement with beauty routines.

The key to understanding choice and constraint in visits to salons and a participation in the beauty industry is to view participation as a complex and unstable interaction between self-view, worldview and *appropriateness*, or as a combination of the working of the habitus within gendered objective structures. Appropriateness is a thoroughly sociological concept. It is where class, age, ethnicity, sexuality and so on enter the discussion. None of the women were in the salon for reasons of beauty. Only outsiders would term salon use as a product of vanity. Instead each client is aiming to achieve a level of bodily performance in accordance with appropriate standards of looking and being. The woman herself occupies a specific social position and moves through a variety of fields. She will invest differentially in the practices available in the salon and outside in order to achieve this level of appropriateness. It is important here not to overemphasise the level of individual and personal choice in the process. However, within her position the woman is able to use the capitals open to her in order to make the best of the resources available. This is one of the meanings of the phrase 'making the best of yourself' often heard in salons. This is perhaps the key process at work in the salon, and it will be returned to in a more theoretical manner below when I discuss 'getting it right'. Self-view and worldview are experienced within a specific historical context. It is to the impact of time upon salon use that I now turn.

Time

In order to begin her salon use the woman must feel that her self-view and worldview allow such a visit, and she must regard her use of the salon as important in achieving some level of 'appropriateness' in relation to her femininity. This process involves a temporal dimension, as the balance between these three areas can shift over time. The narratives of both clients and therapists were full of references to time and to the shifting flow of a life in progress. The life situation of the woman will also vary at different points according to the positions she occupies and the amounts and varieties of capitals she has accrued and is able to capitalise upon. The lifecourse as I am using it here does not imply a linear progression through certain predictable stages of life, but rather the ongoing rebalancing between these factors impacted upon by time and the social spaces occupied. Time is obviously a temporal category, but it is also closely linked to this biographical unfolding (Mills, 1967). Time can be experienced as an immediate concept, as a spatial concept (for example, time in the salon) or as a longer term biographical concept in relation to the lifecourse.

Time in the salon is a not a common experience for all clients, or indeed for all therapists. However, all clients share the experience of time in the salon as being a spatial, social and temporal separation from the world 'outside', a 'change of scenery'. One of the selling points of a visit to the salon is this temporal and spatial 'escape' from everyday life. Depending upon the treatment and the client's reasons for visiting the salon, the time spent there is described in different formats. For example, time expended on regular grooming treatments was described as like 'going to the dentist'. In contrast, Margaret described being in the salon for pampering treatments as 'like a mini holiday'. Time spent in the salon then is both a statement and an activity. This need for spatial removal from the everyday is a key prompt to salon use.

Time in this variety of forms is one of the key factors in influencing if and how the woman will use the beauty salon. Here I break down the concept of time into four categories: lifecourse; turning points; time for myself; and generational change.

Lifecourse

Salon use varies according to the woman's age and her point in the lifecourse. The type of treatment received and the regularity of visits do not remain static over time. It is not necessarily possible to predict how the passage of the lifetime affects salon usage, but in all cases time is a significant factor in influencing the experience of beauty therapy (Furman, 1997). The biography of the individual client does or does not provide spaces within which salon use is appropriate. Economic position and the income available to spend on such commodities also varies. The desire for treatments, however, is the factor most influenced by the lifecourse. Ageing may promote increased visits to the salon as disposable income increases, at the same time as dissatisfaction with bodily appearance brought on by the ageing process or by social demands:

> I'm 35 and I would say the majority of the friends I've got now, we tend to look after ourselves more than they did when they was younger. You could go round with no make-up on and a pair of jeans and a pair of trainers and still look good at 18, 20, but I think as you get older you have got to do more for yourself.
>
> (Anna)

The desire to 'get dressed up' or to receive beauty treatments as a 'change from wearing a sweater with the faint smell of baby sick on the shoulder' (O'Neill, 1993, p. 81) is contingent upon events in the lifecourse. However, it may also be true that increasing age brings with it increased responsibilities in terms of relationships, housing costs and children which militate against salon use. Ageing may also lead to an increasing satisfaction with appearance and bodily being, rather than dissatisfaction and discomfort, and interviewees did mention that they became less concerned with, and less unhappy about, their appearance as they grew older. 'Feeling' treatments may at this point replace the more 'appearance'-orientated treatments and the discourse of justification relating to salon treatments shifts. Ageing may also lead to physical restrictions which necessitate the help of professionals. Lily, a 75-year-old woman receiving a pedicure explains to me:

> You haven't seen me standing up, but I am five foot ten inches and it is such a long way to the end of my legs, and of course with being older, and I was having difficulty cutting my nails, so I decided to come here [salon] and I have been every month since.

The key point here is that salon visits are woven into the biography of the client. The significance of the visits cannot be understood without reference to the biographical situation of the person visiting the salon. Decisions about level of usage, treatment type and importance arise from the everyday life situation of the client and this varies over the lifecourse.

Turning points

Turning points are important biographical ruptures and are often triggers for a change in salon use. Initial visits to salons often centre on holidays, weddings and other special occasions. These turning points are marked by attention to the body and bodily display. The appropriate appearance during each of these transitional phases is achieved through the help of the beauty therapist. Turning points are also transitional phases in terms of social relationships, and again salon visits help to manage these transitions. Turning points may be seen as liminal social spaces or transitional social times where rituals are used to acknowledge the change in status and to smooth the transition. In a late capitalist environment professional expertise may be purchased to manage the disruption.

Preparations for weddings (both the client's own and those of others) is an important function of beauty salons:

> The first time I went [to a salon] as a special occasion. I was going to a wedding and I had a facial done the week before to look my best. I had thought about it before but it took that special occasion.
>
> (Joanne)

Although weddings are important to all social groups, the specifics of the preparations vary according to culture. So, for example, weddings in the UK among people of South Asian origin are elaborate and highly significant. An important part of the preparation for the bride and members of the two families is to undergo beauty treatments. Much of the business among salons catering to a South Asian clientele comes from weddings. Holidays lead to an increase in body hair waxing and other preparations which either alter appearance for this special occasion or save the woman time from routine bodily maintenance tasks while away from home. Holidays serve an important function in management of appearance where the woman is herself, but more so. New styles may be tested out and space is provided to experiment with body image. The purchase and packing of clothes and toiletries is, therefore, a vital aspect of holidays (Banim *et al.*, 2002), as are the preparations undertaken in the beauty salon. Suki was using time during her maternity leave to experiment with a range of massage and other complementary therapies in order to prepare for the birth of her child. This formed a second important period of salon use:

After I got your letter [inviting her to be interviewed] I started thinking about my beauty therapy and I realised that it was after special occasions it happened, the first time I really started to go and it's been sporadic where I've gone intensely for a certain period of time, like my wedding. And then I had a facial done. I had a manicure, pedicure, and I had my wedding make-up done. I think over a period of two months I went quite often and then after that I got married, and then I started to go again and I am pregnant. Since I got pregnant I have had a manicure, a pedicure and a facial.

Turning points then are important triggers for first visits to beauty salons, and for alterations in salon use. However, they are also an aid to narrative construction. When asking interviewees to describe their salon use over time or their experiences of beauty therapy, such turning points are useful in providing a framework within which to construct a narrative. They also offer significant events which act as markers to place memories:

I: Could you tell me a little bit about the first time you went to a salon, do you remember your first visit?
Patricia: God it is ages ago. It was before I had my son and that is ages ago. I can't remember. He is 12 now.

It is not always possible to separate out whether a first visit to a salon occurred before the birth of a first child, or whether the memory is simply placed in this way and produced in narration during the interview, with the birth or other key event acting as an anchor for the story (Passerini, 1989; Rosenthal, 1992).

Time for myself

By claiming time for herself the woman in the salon is making a statement about her own feelings of worth. This claim to time for the self is often a message to partners or others who make demands on the woman's time, and it is also a survival mechanism. Time available for salon visits is both an absolute and relative concept. The client must balance the demands of home life, social relationships and work with their own desire for treatments. At different points in the lifecourse these demands may increase or decrease, or the balance between them may alter.

> I suppose since the children have left home I have more time to myself anyway, whereas when they were at school I got about half an hour to myself because you tend to be doing things for them.
>
> (Judith)

However, interviewees did find time to visit the salon when it became their priority. Carving out a space among the competing demands of others means that sometimes when the woman is most busy seems to be the most necessary time to visit the salon. Mary explains the benefits of time in the salon for women with young children:

> I have lost a lot of confidence and I suppose I am wanting them [salon] to help me build that up. I feel they have fulfilled that role for me really. It is positive and perhaps that is what should be encouraged for women, that when you have children, perhaps that is what you should be given on the NHS. We should all be saying 'no, don't just look to having a cup of tea or whatever, do something for yourself' and this could be a very beneficial way of doing it.

At other points, decreasing priority of salon visits resulted from increased demands in other spheres of their lives. This balancing of multiple demands chimes with the debates around the political economy of time which have quantified and conceptualised what might be commonly understood as the 'rise of the superwoman' (Southerton *et al.*, 2001). In the UK this debate has centred around work/life balance. Since the 1980s in the UK and USA, hours of work have increased, particularly in comparison to other European countries (Fagan, 2002). Childcare provision is not always available to all, varying in accessibility and cost. The vast majority of domestic work is done by women.[1] For these reasons, the time pressures on women have increased, and the claim for time in the salon should be understood in this context. A slightly different context is true for the mythical 'ladies who lunch'. For this segment of the middle class, time in the salon is a display of success. The availability of time away from demands faced by other women is used as an indicator that such labour is carried out by others.

Where time for the self is a priority, visits are often described in terms of pampering, and the discourse of stress is drawn upon to legitimate the need for this escapism. This stress relates to either one area of the woman's life, such as childcare or work commitments, or to managing the competing demands between them:

> I think its rare that I get time to actually treat myself and I see it as something that is completely, solely for me, so it's nice to go and relax and take that time out. I kind of feel like I am owed it as well. I've got to my age, and I've worked and its 'well bloody hell, I should be able to have . . .' and I think also like living in the world that we do where beauty therapy is so apparent and has so much worth attached to it, I don't know, there is a part of me that doesn't want to buy into it, but there is a part of me that does as well. But the most thing [sic] I get out of it is the pampering and the relaxation and the feeling that I've treated myself.
>
> (Rachel)

Stephanie is able to explain her leg waxing as a necessity but is unable to justify other treatments unless she feels that she has 'earned' this time:

> I would like to have a massage done because I think it would be quite relaxing but you feel you have to earn it, but I often think if I have got a lot of teaching on it would be lovely to just relax but then you haven't got time. Then when it's not term time I have got the time but I am not stressed so I don't want to go.

According to Young (1980), discourses of stress have proliferated because they reinforce commonsensical views of human nature. External pressures are unquestioned but accepted, the ability to cope with them understood in individualised terms according to personality or the support mechanisms upon which people are able to draw. Stress has become an amorphous term used as an explanatory tool for a whole range of feelings and behaviours, in this case even justifying recourse to beauty therapy. In the case of the interviewee above, however, this justification is tempered with reluctance.

Marketing and women's media have picked up on this trend towards women claiming 'time for myself'. MacCannell and MacCannell (1987) claim that from the late 1980s the goal of grooming or beauty as described in beauty magazines was transformed. Prior to this date the advice had been geared to achieving a look whose goal was to attract men and to gain a husband. After this point the goal shifted to self-improvement and beauty rituals as a means of achieving satisfaction for the self. Hilary Radner (1989) also pinpoints a shift in advertising of beauty products from the early 1980s. This shift was described by one advertising executive in her study as moving from 'raw sex' (physical appeal to men and achieved for the male gaze) to 'ego-sense'. Ego-sense views the woman as a subject who engages in beauty routines in order to gain pleasure for herself. Time for herself and feeling that 'she is worth it' are common refrains within this new approach to advertising.

> The most marked transition in the representation of women in advertising was from the portrayal of the domestically oriented woman to a woman who sought to please herself. Femininity was no longer exclusively defined through the representation of male desire, in which feminine desire was figured as the desire for male desire. Femininity began to be formulated as the construction of a feminine subject that, as a woman, wanted and desired *like* a man, but not *as* a man.
>
> (Radner, 1989, p. 302; emphasis in original)

What has happened in advertising and in women's magazines is a rearticulation of beauty products and make-up away from activities which are aimed towards the male gaze, and towards seeing these products and activities as something the woman engages in *for herself*. Claiming time for the self then is both a temporal concept and a justificatory discourse which chimes with processes of individualisation – the woman is responsible for her own children, her own career, her health and the happiness of her partner. In her investigation of Ann Summers parties,[2] Storr claims that women's participation in such events offers 'pleasure and self-esteem' while leaving socio-economic inequalities unchallenged. In this sense she argues that the Ann Summers party plan should be thought of as a post-feminist organisation (Storr, 2003, p. 30). Although I do not argue that beauty salons can be understood in exactly the same way, the women in this study responded to their own individual responsibilities by escaping to the salon in search of 'pleasure and self-esteem'. Ironically, the type of salon use and the practices carried out there are thoroughly socially embedded.

Generational change

One of the questions the interviewees were asked was about the use of beauty salons within their family, and whether beauty salon visits would have been something undertaken by their mothers (or fathers). Where interviewees had children they were also questioned about their daughters' attitudes towards dress, make-up and beauty. Two women described occasions in their early teens where their mothers had paid for their own salon visits. Christina had suffered badly from acne and her mother had viewed the salon visits as an accompaniment to medical treatment for the skin condition. Justification for these visits then was made through a discourse of health. Lisa, a woman with pale skin and dark hair, described how her mother had encouraged visits to the salon for removal of body hair. Her mother had encouraged its removal, viewing this dark body hair as a symbol of masculinity. The justification here was made in terms of grooming in that smooth skin was seen as necessary, and waxing viewed as the method that would cause least problems for the girl later in life. However, management of the symbols of ethnicity is a clear undercurrent here, as dark hair against pale skin was seen as being less acceptable than fair hair might have been. Thus hair 'out of place' becomes a symbol of both masculinity and ethnicity.

With the exception of this one interviewee whose mother and friends regularly attended beauty salons in an affluent area of the southeast of England, beauty salon visits were generally agreed to be something which had become more common among women in recent times. Women in their twenties and thirties especially felt that their own beauty routines were significantly different to those of an earlier generation. In terms of the amount of time spent on beauty routines, on the products consumed and salon visits, these women believed that they devoted more time, effort and disposable income to their own beauty routines than their mothers had done. All agreed that there had been an increase in the number of beauty salons to cater for this increased demand, but also partly acting as a stimulus to demand. These changes were explained in terms of women's freedom to spend both time and their own money on themselves. Beauty salon visits were seen as part of a leisure and service industry catering to the needs of women who were independent in both their financial and personal decisions.

Beauty therapists too explain the increase in their business in these terms. The expanding leisure industry and the commodification of beauty rituals to an ever-increasing extent have contributed to the professionalisation of the salon, which has in turn altered the behaviour of women from one generation to the next:

> I think years ago there was almost not a sort of business ethic behind beauty therapy. It was a kind of luxurious service. And I think it was a lot of small salons working on quite outmoded and outdated lines and were seen very much as a wealthy woman's option. I think it has changed quite radically. . . . Now it is a lot slicker, more business oriented. Salons seem to plan a little better, analyse what they are doing to maximise their market. The bigger companies are a

big influence. I think it's the growth of the leisure industry that has dragged us forward because, you know, the hotels are now big business, and gyms in hotels. So now we have a lot of salons in hotels alongside the leisure complex. . . . And I think it is far more accessible to people. With the advent of the fitness regime and people going to gyms and being more concerned and that, they are more exposed to beauty therapy and they are thinking well why not? I have worked out in the gym, why not treat myself to a massage? Why not have a facial?

(Amanda BT)

This transformation in the nature of the salon tells us much about the commodification of the body and the corporatisation of body practices. The early development of the salon (discussed in Chapter 2) relied heavily on the entrepreneurship of individual women in local contexts. Although some of them, for example, Madam C. J. Walker, went on to develop an extensive business empire, the roots of most salons were female-owned, locally based, small-scale shops. In contrast, the salon of today is more likely to be owned and operated by a large multinational company less sensitive to local idiosyncrasies. This is not to deny that this sector still provides a significant amount of female employment and women-owned and run businesses. However, even in small salons large multinationals set the standard of operation, they distribute advertising, they are the suppliers of products to the salon, and they are involved in training and accreditation processes. It would be very difficult for current beauty salon clients to avoid the effects of this influence.

Women were also seen to be increasingly subject to pressure to appear groomed and to maintain certain levels of appearance. This pressure is filtered through the media and other cultural forms, as well as being one of the regulations operating in the workplace. This also feeds back into the personal freedoms experienced by these women. With freedom comes the pressure to succeed. By being part of the 'can have it all' generation, they felt that they were expected to 'have it all', and appearance was a key indicator of success in important if limited terms:

Clare: My mum always said to me, 'Oh you can do whatever you want with your life'. But that is like a massive pressure isn't it? Because I could have done anything and look what I have done. I haven't done anything. Oh God I am such a failure! Do you know what I mean? But I think lots of our generation are like that, like we are really miserable because like beating our heads against a brick wall because we are not something that we should be but are not really sure what it is because we don't know what we want.

I: Do you think having that ideal of what we should start off as is part of the whole problem?

Clare: Yes because you have got the house, the apartment, the career, you have got to be gorgeous because we can have it all.

This pressure experienced by young women in particular was one of the impulses for beauty salon use. This generation has grown up in an environment of what has been termed 'post-feminism'. The gains made by feminism such as access to free and safe contraception and a commitment to equality in the workplace, at least in the affluent industrial world, mean that young women have been freed up to make choices regarding occupation and sexuality within less rigid restrictions than their mothers. However, this freedom has also been experienced as responsibility and fear of failure. This group of women have also rejected the strict dichotomy between feminism and femininity which characterised popular understandings of feminism in the 1970s and1980s (Moseley and Read, 2002). Using the example of the TV programme *Ally McBeal*, Moseley and Read argue that the choices made by young women in the UK and USA are drawn from an agenda set by feminism, but that the rejection of beauty culture and femininity previously associated with the feminist movement has been reworked. Young women believe, therefore, that they can 'have it all', and that this entails career, economic independence, property owning, sexual freedom, and investment in a feminine appearance. The freedom and fun to be had by gaining these rewards is also a pressure to succeed with all of them. What I think is missing from Moseley and Read's discussion, however, is an acknowledgement that the desire to achieve a feminised body is the product of a commodified system. As Oullette points out in her examination of the effect the editorial policy of Helen Gurley Brown had on the magazine *Cosmopolitan*: 'By the time Brown's *Cosmopolitan* appeared in 1965, womanly perfection was dependent on the ongoing purchase of the consumer products advertised in the magazines' (Oullette, 1999, p. 365). Interestingly, Gurley Brown advocated that these consumption practices be used to purchase the symbols of cultural capital which would propel the woman into upward mobility, most often through marriage to a middle-class man. For the new 'career woman' the services of the beauty therapy industry facilitate the achievement of an appropriate femininity, but at a cost. The desire to have it all is fostered within a liberal market economy. With sufficient levels of disposable income the young woman buys leisure and pleasure from industries geared up to convince her that she has failed without them.

Although unusual, there was some comment on this process among clients:

> I think that there is a generation of women who are university educated who were brought up not directly by their mothers but the generation above to have certain opinions of what women should be, and they were quite strongly ingrained opinions, which is where my thinking came from, constantly reading feminist-type novels gave me strongly ingrained views. I am a teacher and I don't think any of my pupils have it. And I think there is not one girl in my sixth form who isn't absolutely plastered in make-up. I don't think there is one girl who says you shouldn't shave your legs, that is conforming to the particular type of femininity. They would just laugh at you.
>
> (Laura)

When I later questioned Laura about the effects she thought this had on these young women, she replied that they would 'probably be happier and less angst ridden than our generation'.

The developing interest of children in body and beauty was also acknowledged by those women with daughters. Although generally indulging this interest and comparing it to dressing up or experimenting with appearance and identity, the boundaries of this feminised image were carefully policed by the mothers:

Fiona: My daughter went to a friend's house and she came back and her face was made up and I just thought, no.

I: How old was she?

Fiona: She must have been about five then. I just thought, no. I said it looks horrible and I took her in the bathroom and washed it off, and the nail varnish. It just rang bells of child pornography, stuff like that. I took a picture of her and I got the picture back and looked at it and ripped it up. It just looked awful.

Generational change was acknowledged both between clients and their own parents, and between themselves and their daughters. The levels of both freedoms and pressures upon the lives of women were seen as contributing to this change, and these were seen to feed into interest in beauty matters.

Getting into the salon is a process which involves work on the self and the achievement of a resonance between self-view and worldview. This process is temporal in that biographical factors impact on the time available to the woman, and also the potential she has to claim 'time for herself' among other competing demands. It is also placed within a specific historical context. The work of understanding the role of the beauty salon begins before the woman enters its doors.

Getting it right

So now the woman has become a beauty salon client, what exactly is she trying to achieve through her visits? It is impossible here to overemphasise the importance of *appropriateness*. This 'getting it right' is the key to understanding not only beauty salon visits or the operation of the wider beauty industry, but also for making sense of women's relationship to ideals of femininity. The notion of appropriateness not only varies with time, as I have outlined above, but also with space. I will discuss the geographical and social spaces within which appropriate gender performance is achieved below.

Here I am using appropriateness as both a participant concept and a more highly theorised concept. Therapists and clients all speak of what is suitable for the client, or what would 'look right', what would 'suit her' and other similar phrases. This is one area where the therapist can exercise her professional expertise in advising the client, or in simply carrying out treatments in a manner she believes to be in the client's best interests. The client too will negotiate with the therapist over desired outcomes. However, I am also theorising this empirical concept in specifically feminist terms. In order to do this I draw on the work of Bourdieu, but moderate his approach in order to fully take into account other characteristics besides class. It is a familiar criticism of Bourdieu that his schema prioritises class at the expense of gender and ethnicity. Particularly in his early writings, where gender is referred to, it is done so in the manner of sexual difference (Mottier, 2002). Bourdieu published *Masculine Domination* (2001) partly as a response to these criticisms, although he claims that 'I would probably not have embarked on such a difficult subject if I had not been compelled to do so by the whole logic of my research' (2001, p. 1). However, in this book, despite taking full account of gender, Bourdieu manages to virtually ignore the feminist literature of the past thirty years. In understanding appropriateness I will use Bourdieu's work but I will also draw upon the work of feminist authors.

Before I begin, however, I believe it is worth making a point concerning the nature of the sample on which my arguments are based. Although I would argue that appropriateness is a concept which has broad application, and which may be used to understand the pleasures and dangers of investing in femininity, I should also strike a note of caution. All of the women included in this study are either beauty therapists or clients of beauty salons. As such they represent a sample which by its very nature is highly committed to achieving a desired outcome as a result of their investment in beauty/body practices. This means that they are likely to possess a heightened sense of (bodily) appropriateness. The concern about appearance and the fear hovering in the background of a concept such as appropriateness is perhaps to some extent exaggerated by focusing on women who invest time and disposable income in their bodies in this way.

In Bourdieu's relational view of gender, the social world is dichotomised into symbols which relate to the male and the female. The bodies of men and women too form part of this relational set of symbols. In fact the division of bodies into sexes is a *product* of this gendered system: 'The social world constructs the body as a sexually defined reality and as the depository of sexually defining principles of vision and division' (Bourdieu, 2001, p. 11). This division is seen as natural and its naturalness is reinforced through the *doxa*, or the taken-for-grantedness of sexual division. 'Everybody knows' that there are men and women, and divisions between bodies are drawn on to support this doxic view. The imposition of femininity upon women is achieved through what Bourdieu terms *symbolic violence*:

> I have seen masculine domination, and the way it is imposed and suffered, as the prime example of this paradoxical submission, an effect of what I call symbolic violence, a gentle violence, imperceptible and invisible even to its victims, exerted for the most part through the purely symbolic channels of communication and cognition (more precisely, misrecognition), recognition, or even feeling. This extraordinarily ordinary social relation thus offers a privileged opportunity to grasp the logic of the domination exerted in the name of a symbolic principle known and recognized both by the dominant and by the dominated – a language (or a pronunciation),

a lifestyle (or a way of thinking, speaking and acting) – and, more generally, a distinctive property, whether emblem or stigma.

(Bourdieu, 2001, pp. 1–2)

Through the habitus, or the internalisation of objective social structures, women come to make choices which are constrained by their gendered identity. I have discussed the habitus in more depth in relation to the processes which occur prior to salon use. Here the habitus is useful for understanding the nature of symbolic violence:

> Symbolic violence is a subtle, euphemized, invisible mode of domination that prevents domination from being recognized as such and, therefore, as misrecognized domination, is socially recognized. It works when subjective structures – the habitus – and objective structures are in accord with each other.
>
> (Krais, 1993, p. 172)

While agreeing with the power of symbolic violence, and the power exerted when the habitus and objective structures align to produce this domination, what I find interesting are the spaces allowed where habitus and social structures are imperfectly aligned. In fact it could be argued that a perfect alignment is never possible. Psychoanalytical work has shown how femininity is not an easy role to adopt, or one which is ever fully achieved (Rose, 1983). Neither objective structures nor the habitus can ever form a unified monolithic totality. Contradictions exist both within and between them. The tensions between the internalised standards of female gender and their expression through the body are one example. The ambivalence exhibited by the women in this study to their own investment in feminised bodily capital illustrates such spaces. Spaces for critique can emerge, for example, from class position, from a feminist-inspired criticism of the gender order, from a sense of racial politics, or from a non-heterosexual identity.

Complicity on the part of the dominated is inevitable in the sense that the operation of the habitus is unconscious and the choices presented through the habitus are constrained by the social order:

> 'Complicity' implies, then, that the person who is confronted by acts of symbolic violence is disposed to perceive the violence in these acts, to decode relevant signals, and to understand their veiled social meaning, but without recognizing them consciously as what they are – namely, as words, gestures, movements, and intonations of domination.
>
> (Krais, 1993, p. 172)

The complicity of the woman in her femininity is inevitable, since she has inescapably grown up in a society based on a gendered hierarchy. She has also acquired a gendered habitus which guides her speech, her taste, her way of understanding and relating to the world, and her very sense of being.

However, the complicity is never complete as we are never only a gendered subject. It is impossible to separate out the aspects of my identity which relate to other social positions besides my gender. The attempt to do so has led too often to a biological reductionist approach. The complicity understood by Bourdieu is also a basis for struggle. If we take the example of 'race' we can see how the dominated are represented by, and come to see themselves in the eyes of, the dominated:

> It is a peculiar consciousness this sense of always looking at one's self through the eyes of others, of measuring one's soul by the tape of a world that looks on in amused contempt and pity. One ever feels his two-ness.
>
> (Du Bois, in Gates and Oliver, 1999, p. 11)

This understanding leads to complicity with the dominant view, but also resistance to it.

The understanding of the ambivalent femininities being striven for in the beauty salon must arise from the sense that all women inhabit a society based on gendered and unequal objective social structures, and have internalised a gendered habitus. Despite this inevitably gendered position, the woman also inhabits objective social structures which are hierarchical in relation to class, ethnicity and sexuality. These are also incorporated into the habitus. She also moves between various fields and accrues a variety of capitals. We will return to this movement in space below. For all of these reasons the woman is able to both embrace and reject an idealised femininity. The achievement of appropriateness is a reflection of this process.

A further criticism of Bourdieu which enables us to understand the ambivalences inherent in gender identity is the fact that he too easily dichotomises gender. For Bourdieu, male and female, masculine and feminine, are constantly referred back to his field-work with the Kabyle, and from here to a fundamental structuring principle of understanding. In *Masculine Domination*, his picture of gendered identities is too simplistic in its portrayal of the man and the woman learning what it is to be female and male. There is little room for variations within the sex categories. As Connell has pointed out, masculinity may be seen as an internally frag-mented category which is historically contingent (Connell, 1995). Bourdieu takes little account of the contradictions within gendered identities which might allow women to form differentially gen-dered habituses. For this reason the woman in the salon is in a no-win situation. Femininity demands that she pay attention to her appearance and achieve a state acceptable within carefully defined boundaries. However, her investment in femininity con-signs her to a lower social status, forever associated with the body and with nature.

Bourdieu's schema is useful to understand the relative stability of masculine domination, and also in illustrating how such a system does not need explicit violence to maintain unequal power struc-tures. His concept of symbolic violence allows us to understand the 'complicity' of the dominated. In a much less ambitious pro-posal I am attempting to draw on Bourdieu, and feminist-inspired critiques of his work, to understand how women are both com-plicit and ambiguous about their own investments in gendered bodily appearance. In order to do so I will elaborate upon the term *appropriateness*.

I am using the term 'appropriateness' in a manner very close to how Bev Skeggs has used 'respectability' (Skeggs, 1997). Respectability for her is the yardstick against which working-class women are measured but constantly and inevitably found wanting: 'Respectability has always been a marker and a burden of class, a standard to which to aspire' (Skeggs, 1997, p. 3). The dangers of being a 'slag', of 'letting yourself go' or of being 'scruffy' are a constant presence in the narratives of the working-class women she describes. However, by the very fact of their gender and class position, those women can never attain true respectability in that this belongs to the individualised bourgeois subject alone: 'Respectability became a property of middle-class individuals defined against the masses' (ibid., p. 3).

The women's relationship to obtaining this respectability is, as Skeggs clearly shows, ultimately ambivalent. They are aware of their own pathologisation through discourses which position them as 'deviant'. However, this understanding is not accepted passively. Their ambivalence in striving for, yet at the same time rejecting and ridiculing, the signifiers of 'respectable' middle-class femininity ensures that these women cannot be seen either as 'cultural dopes' or as unambiguously oppressed by an all-powerful beauty system engaged in some form of backlash against the advances made by middle-class women (Wolf, 1990):

> The women of this study are not just ciphers from which subject positions can be read-off; rather, they are active in producing the meaning of the positions they (refuse to, reluctantly or willingly) inhabit.
>
> (Skeggs, 1997, p. 2)

It is in this sense that the women in Skeggs' study are actively and complexly negotiating their own relationships with gender identity. This concept of respectability works wonderfully to grasp the pains of 'failure', of 'getting it wrong', but also to express the joy and the humour of never fully 'buying into' bourgeois individual subjectivity. However, my own use of appropriateness is different to Skeggs' respectability in two key ways. This difference in approach is partly related to methodology. The women in Skeggs' study were all white, they were drawn from a similar class background, a compact geographical location, and all were initially enrolled on a similar course at a local college. The clients and therapists in this study were drawn from wider geographical, cultural and economic backgrounds. Although not a large proportion of the sample, black and Asian women are also included. It is therefore inevitable that concepts based on these differing groups of women will result in a different emphasis.

My first disagreement with Skeggs is that although her work is very carefully grounded in an empirical setting which shows how the 'hidden injuries of class' are worked out on a day-to-day level, her categorisation of the pathologisation of white working-class femininity relies too heavily on a monolithic concept of middle-class culture and identity. As I have discussed above, there is a tension between different categorisations of middle-class femininity, for example, between what I have called 'career women' and 'ladies who lunch'. Although according to a variety of class schema both of these groups of women would be placed into a category of middle class, their specific position is very different. Such differences undermine the extent to which 'bourgeois femininity' can be seen as an unproblematic and monolithic concept. The expansions of the service industry and transformations in post-war education have helped to create what has been called the 'service class'. Although a heated debate centres on the nature and role of this hypothesised class, what commentators do acknowledge is that this professional and managerial sector has expanded rapidly in the UK during the twentieth and early twenty-first centuries (Butler, 1995). Savage *et al.* (1992) have postulated divisions even within this stratum and divide its members according to access to 'property, bureaucracy and culture' (Butler, 1995, p. 34). For this reason, although I agree with Skeggs concerning the pathologisation of working-class womanhood, I differ in the extent to which I would also wish to problematise conflicting femininities within classes. In fact the segmentation within the beauty market reflects these divisions.

Second, appropriateness also differs from respectability in that to some extent I am using it to cut across class divisions to relate to femininity *per se*. I want to be very clear here, however, that I am not rejecting Skeggs' arguments that the achievements of femininity are class based. I feel it is useful to make use of a term which is able to look at the bodily practices of all women, while at the same time allowing for the very different potentialities dependent upon position. So, for example, appropriateness varies according to space and time. However, for all women who wish to achieve an appropriate heterosexual feminine bodily disposition, facial hair is always and everywhere considered disruptive to this aim. Facial hair itself becomes a signifier of either a rejection of this appropriate femininity, or a disengagement with it. To display bodily symbols of unfemininity is to enter the realms of the abject:

> This exclusionary matrix by which subjects are formed thus requires the simultaneous production of a domain of abject beings, those who are not yet 'subjects', but who form the constitutive outside to the domain of the subject. The abject designates here precisely those 'unlivable' and 'uninhabitable' zones of social life which are nevertheless populated by those who do not enjoy the status of the subject, but whose living under the sign of the 'unlivable' is required to circumscribe the domain of the subject.
>
> (Butler, 1993, p. 3)

In some ways then appropriateness cuts across class position in applying to gender and femininity. For example, Amanda describes the anguish of clients with facial hair:

> When you do a consultation there's two things a woman will always say. She will always say – jokingly – 'I thought I was turning into a man'. But it is a fundamental worry that they're losing their femininity. . . . So they are convinced that they are on their own and they are convinced that they are no longer feminine. It's an awful thing for a woman to feel like that, very, very damaging. And they feel isolated because it's not

anything you can talk to somebody else about. You can't say, 'Oh, how do you deal with your beard?' I knew one woman who used to get up, religiously, half an hour before her husband, go to the bathroom, tweeze out all the hair on her chin, put on full make-up before her husband was up. He didn't know she had a problem.

(Amanda BT)

This fear of 'turning into a man' is a very real sensation for women undergoing removal of facial hair. The beauty salon is made use of to police the boundaries of an 'acceptable' bodily state. However, the fear of gender ambiguity exhibited here is more akin to Bartky's 'threat of annihilation' (Bartky, 1997, p. 105) than Butler's ironic and transgressive acts.

The understanding of treatments in relation to gender in this way is also a critique of Bourdieu's prioritisation of class-based habitus. Within the habitus contradictions may exist. For example, the idealised standard of white middle-class femininity may co-exist with a critique of the racism inherent in such norms (Weekes, 1997; Craig, 2002). Paradoxes also exist in the ways in which women are expected to behave and to look appropriate. While heterosexual women of certain ages are exhorted to appear sexually attractive, they are also admonished for being sexually available. The dubious 'justification' in cases of sexual attack that 'she was asking for it' testifies to this dangerous paradox in the achievement of femininity. This paradox becomes even more dangerous in a racist culture which sexualises black female bodies (hooks, 1982). The very category of woman is a subordinated identity leading to the impossibility of achieving a successful feminine identity. To achieve femininity and to invest in it may gain some limited rewards and avoid sanction, but the association with femininity means that it remains a subordinated identity despite its privileges over other identities at times.

My concept of appropriateness then allows for tensions and differences within classes, and also for an understanding of some aspects of gender which cross-cut purely class-based schema. However, I am not stating here that femininity can make sense in isolation, without reference to class, ethnicity and other factors. Indeed, how appropriateness works out in different local empirical contexts, and in a wider theoretical framework which articulates both class and gender, is a crucial question.

The overarching concept of appropriateness as I am using it in this study is made up of three specific areas. Each area is based closely on client interviews but has been theorised according to my own conceptual schema. Women require *knowledge* of what is appropriate, they require *skill* in order to achieve their goals and they must also be able to engage in a *performance* which displays the achievement of appropriateness if they are to avoid sanction and ridicule. All these processes may be undertaken without the help of the beauty professional, or with the help of professionals of another kind (e.g. hairdressers, beauticians, clothing shop assistants). However, in all of these spheres the woman is constantly negotiating her own relationship to femininity in relation to both inner (self-view and worldview, or the habitus) and outer (position) influences. This does not necessarily require a conscious decision-making process but may simply be seen as the ongoing negotiation between knowledge, skill and performance, all of which can operate at either a conscious or automatic level.

Knowledge

Knowledge of appropriateness comes from a number of sources, some explicit and others implicit. Beauty therapists and the wider beauty industry serve as sources of information for both beauty salon clients and others. Beauty therapists act as sources of advice for particular treatments within the salon. They also offer products for sale and may recommend either specific treatments or products in addition to those already purchased by the client. It is here that the therapist acts as both cultural interpreter and saleswoman. She also provides a source of knowledge on the appropriateness of any particular treatment. This appropriateness is in two senses. First, the therapist is trained to have detailed knowledge of most if not all of the treatments offered in the salon. She knows the benefits of the treatment and also any contraindications. She is an expert in providing the correct treatment for the outcome desired. In this way her professional expertise facilitates decisions made by the client in terms of selecting appropriate treatments. However, the therapist also acts as an arbitrator in terms of an aesthetic appropriateness. In treatments such as the application of make-up, or eyebrow shaping, the therapist is making judgements about the aesthetic outcome in terms of a set of criteria which relate as much to the age, ethnicity and so on of the client, as to any professional expertise:

> Make-up is so subjective and what you think would look good on somebody is not their perception of what looks good on themselves. Students start out by putting their own make-up on everybody, which a 60-year-old lady will not always suit! . . . They won't say 'I hate it', but you know that they go into the toilet before they go home and take off all that the student has put on, because its a young person's make-up that has gone on to someone who really shouldn't be wearing so much make-up.
>
> (Gillian BT)

Beauty therapists will also advise clients on a particular 'look' which suits them. This is generally offered only when the client has requested such advice:

> You see in magazines and they say you do this and you do that, but I think do I really know? Am I wearing the right colours? Am I putting this on right? And the answers were no, no, no, no you are not. . . . She [therapist] did go through that I was wearing the wrong colour foundation – I was wearing something too dark. I had got a feeling that maybe it wasn't quite right and she said it wasn't right.
>
> (Bridget)

However, advice is sometimes offered even when not requested. During one conversation with three therapists in Yvette's salon I was asked my age. On replying, I noticed glances passed between them and it was remarked that 'Paula should start on her neck'! The perceived intimacy of the client–therapist relationship sometimes facilitates the offering of unsolicited advice.

Although the therapist acts as a source of knowledge for clients in the salon, there are many more widely disseminated and ultimately more powerful sources of such knowledge. The media and other cultural forms serve as a key source of information concerning not only the treatments and products available to women and men consumers, but also information regarding what is fashionable and appropriate to the consumer's social positioning:

> Yes, there are always these magazines with gorgeous women staring back at you. You think that's the way men perceive you as, and that's the way you should look yourself.
>
> (Nathalie BT)

In this quote Nathalie is referring to a generalised aesthetic rather than to a specific set of guidelines or advice. She also associates this aesthetic with the male gaze reproduced in and through the media. Women's magazines crammed with beauty advice and advertising are scattered around the waiting rooms of beauty salons. The women in this study also read these magazines, often ambivalently, but also aspirationally. The ever-increasing popularity of 'make-over' shows on TV also attest to the hunger for information on what to wear, what to buy, and how not to get caught out looking somehow 'wrong'.

A hugely popular show on British TV in recent years is called *What Not to Wear*. In this programme two presenters, Trinny and Susannah, respond to members of the public who have nominated an acquaintance as a candidate for a 'make-over'. The unsuspecting subject of the show is initially secretly filmed going about their everyday business while the presenters comment on her dress, hair and make-up. After we have witnessed this embarrassing spectacle the candidate is confronted and offered a sum of money to replace her wardrobe, but only if she follows Trinny and Susannah's advice. The humiliation does not end there. The 'star' of the programme is then invited into offices with her clothes and shoes. She is placed in a cubicle with mirrors all around and forced to view herself (critically) from every angle. This wonderfully Foucauldian moment usually removes all resistance to the exercise. The woman then goes on a shopping spree following the 'rules' set by the presenters and appears transformed at the end of the programme. A follow-up video tracks her adherence to the newly imposed rules of fashion, and the presenters despair over any relapses to the original offending sense of style.

There are several interesting features of this programme. It has picked up on a trend in 'real-life' shows popular with the British TV viewing public. It is also part of a series of programmes which give advice on how to style the home, the garden, the body, and even go so far as to offer advice on how to hold dinner parties in a way which conforms to strict standards of etiquette. The 'experts' in these programmes derive some of their legitimacy from their ability to translate 'good taste' into a modified sensibility applicable to those who do not occupy such an elevated social standing. Most of the subjects of *What Not to Wear* are white women, although some shows have been devoted to white men. The use of the panoptical chamber at the beginning of the show is a master stroke in TV making which forces subjects to confront the 'truth' of their own lack of taste. Their dress sense is ridiculed as making them look too old, too fat or too cheap. The presenters Trinny and Susannah can only be described as what one would call, in the UK, 'posh'. Their names, their accents and their modes of dress and grooming all indicate that they originate from an upper-middle-class background. This show has caught the UK *Zeitgeist* in playing on fears, most keenly felt by women, of 'getting it wrong' in their dress. Trinny and Susannah happily talk about 'tits' and 'arses' while imposing a sanitised and class-based taste schema on their usually pliable and grateful victims.

Despite such programmes it would be highly simplistic to argue, as I have heard undergraduate students sometimes do, that 'the media create eating disorders' or that young women undertake various body modifications due to media images in their turn being translated into 'peer pressure'. There is now a vast amount of media attention aimed at women and men, and the body has increasingly become commodified both in terms of its use in media and advertising and as a target for consumption. However, it is not the case that these media images in themselves can be said to have such a devastating impact. Rather, the social situatedness of knowledge about what is appropriate translates these messages into consumption and body practices which make sense within the specific social position occupied by the woman. Choosing what looks and feels right for any occasion is guided by everyday social relationships, but also by the exercise of a particular taste (Bourdieu, 1984, 1993). It is this taste which remains at the level of the taken for granted and guides consumption choices beneath our level of consciousness.

Knowledge concerning what looks right, the correct clothes to wear for differing social engagements, the acceptable length and colour of nails, knowing that it is unacceptable to wear miniskirts with unshaved or unwaxed legs is experienced and policed within social relationships. This is the very stuff of human life within which the woman exists on a day-to-day level. The intensity, duration and intimacy of relationships vary, but all are key in providing this knowledge and in policing the boundaries of its application. So, for example, women at work might compare which salons they visit and the types of treatments offered. They might complement each other on a particular change of hairstyle, manicure or shade of lipstick. Alternatively, in the case of strained relationships with work colleagues, failure to make such appreciative comments is a symbol of that difficult relationship and a subtle form of conflict. Friends offer opinions during shopping trips on the style of clothes most suited to the woman. Mothers comment on the daughter's need to take better care of her skin, or make disapproving remarks about the amount of money spent on beauty products. Knowledge then is not simply cognitive, it is the internalised result of social relationships and social position.

Skill

In order to achieve both the looks and the behaviour of appropriateness a certain level of skill is required. Throughout her life a woman learns how to behave in appropriate ways. Her body is disciplined in the feminine modes of speech, walking, sitting and so on (Young, 1980). The woman learns the methods of washing and conditioning hair, and how to style it using a variety of products. She also learns how to dress appropriately for a variety of situations and in a way that fits with her own self-image and her appropriate position. In beauty terms she learns how to cleanse, tone and moisturise, the three-step programme marketed for skin maintenance. As a young girl these routines were sold to me in *Jackie,* a magazine aimed at girls which contained picture stories, advice columns and features on fashion and beauty (McRobbie, 1991). The rituals of feminine bodily care/discipline are today also passed on in magazines aimed at young women (Walkerdine, 1997). Women then are adept at shaving, cleansing, moisturising, deodorising and painting their already shaped bodies (Holland *et al.*, 1994). As if to reinforce the amount of work which goes into such skills, and the constant vigilance required to update them, Mary (client) describes how an accident several years earlier had led to her withdrawal from the labour market. At the time of our interview she had been visiting a salon in order to prepare for a return to paid employment:

> [I am] tying to rebuild this woman and get her back into the workforce. I am not sure it will ever happen or am I totally ruined now? Four years down the line and will I ever work again? I am trying to look at what other women do because once you fall out of the workforce, four or five years ago people wore business suits. People don't dress like that anymore, and you do lose that – you lose the ability to look just part of them, the working population.

The visits to the salon here are an attempt to refamiliarise herself with the skills required to produce a feminine groomed appearance. Despite receiving a confidence boost, she did feel that treatments in the salon were insufficient to fully provide this service.

It could be questioned whether what women are doing can properly be labelled skills. Jeffries, for example, argues that it is not appropriate to elevate the tasks of the sex worker above the work carried out by other heterosexual women. In attempting to validate their work as requiring specialised skills, she argues, we are simply reinforcing women's association with a demeaning and ultimately harmful industry (Jeffries, 1997). A parallel could be drawn to women's engagement in beauty rituals and to the work of therapists. Other commentators have argued that the corporeal practices engaged in by women require a significant amount of skill and draw upon a detailed knowledge of the body (Radner, 1989). However, even if we concede a highly developed set of skills, the woman can claim no form of recognition or reward for them. This is, as I have already stated, because such work on the body strengthens an association with the corporeal and the natural, reinforcing the inferiority of women's skills and knowledge (Grosz, 1994; Bartky, 1990). It seems one of the ultimate ironies to me that gendered bodies can be regarded as natural and the result of birth, while at the same time so much work is obviously carried out on them to maintain this 'natural' state. For the woman, 'looking good' is interpreted as an immanent feminine characteristic, naturalised and unremarkable (Adkins, 2001). She is unable to convert this type of skill into any form of recognised capital. In order for any skill to be rewarded it must be valued and recognised. This symbolic capital depends for its existence on a process of recognition (Skeggs, 2001). Both skills and the recognition of them are context specific and so, while the failure to engage in the rituals of femininity certainly draws sanction, developing the skills necessary to become fully feminine does not ensure reward.

The beauty therapist is also caught in this no-win situation. Her professional competencies relate to traditional female qualities such as caring, listening and corporeal intimacy, thereby partly negating any claims to professional expertise gained through rigorous training (Willett, 2000; Sharma and Black, 2001). It is the beauty therapist's role to offer her services to clients who cannot achieve their desired outcome by themselves. She is also recruited where time constraints and convenience mean that it is preferable for the woman to buy in the skills of others. In some cases the beauty therapist may offer skills which the woman herself does not possess, or where the required outcome is not obtainable to the same standard through self-treatment. Waxing is one example where clients are unable to achieve similar results to a salon treatment, or are afraid of the pain experienced to such an extent that the therapist's services are called upon. In some cases the therapist may be seen as an expert even where the woman does have the skills to treat herself. Eyebrow shaping is an oft-cited example where women feel that the looks achieved are preferable from the salon than by their own efforts even though the process itself is similar in both instances. This level of skill is an integral part of the routines of femininity, the very essence of being a woman. Although some women may claim to have no knowledge of such skills, and to be unpractised in carrying them out, this simply exhibits an ambivalent relationship to practising them. In fact most women have been exposed to this knowledge and skill in the very process of growing up female.

Performance

The third characteristic of appropriateness is that it requires a performance to display the knowledge and skills developed in the process of becoming female, and also that performance is necessary to show that appropriateness is being achieved. Performance is a vital aspect of the bodily being of women and men in that it refers to the doing and being of gender identity. It relates to both a surface display and a more deeply embedded way of being in the world. In this sense it operates at the conscious level of 'getting it right' but also at a more automatic level of everyday taken for grantedness.

Performance as it arises from the interviews with beauty salon clients and therapists is a display and a showing, and is more easily understood in this context as relating to 'looking treatments' such as the removal of facial hair or the more mainstream 'beauty' treatments. The return from holiday sporting a tan symbolises leisure, escapism and health. The manicure and facial prior to a wedding show that the guest has realised the importance of the event and is doing her best to respect the traditions of the occasion. Eyebrow plucking and eyelash tinting save time in the mornings when preparing for work, but they also indicate that the necessity for a smart or groomed appearance in the workplace has been accepted. In response to my question about the importance of her manicures Anna (who worked as door staff in a night-club) explains:

> Why is it so important? Because I do a male's job at night and I like to look feminine doing the job as well, still to look like a female actually doing the job.

She goes on to justify her desire for false eyelashes:

> You look at people's eyes all the time, they get noticed don't they? Whoever they are, male or female, so the eyes are always emphasised I think. I don't know, I think I might look more attractive or more eye-catching to somebody if I've got longer eyelashes.

The sense of show is explicit in her justifications for salon treatments to an extent not always evident in client narratives. However, there is always present a desire to work on their gendered appearance. Even when visits to the salon are kept secret, the performance of a gendered identity is present in the stories told by clients. Patricia explains how she does not tell anyone about her electrolysis to remove facial hair, stating, 'I'm just embarrassed I suppose'. She goes on to say that:

> I've never had a beauty treatment or whatever. It's just not me. It doesn't bother me if I didn't have a facial or a massage, it doesn't bother me.

However, she sees her electrolysis as a necessity:

> I would have to find it [the money for treatment]. I would have to take it out of something else and use it for that. Whatever bill, and the bill would have to come later. I would have to find the money.

This treatment for her is not something to be discussed with others, but the results are dramatic in their effect on her demeanour, emotions and deportment:

I: How do you feel when you leave the salon?
Patricia: Oh, I hold my head up and my chin up. It makes you feel good because you can face people. When I face people I don't have to hold my head down or hide behind my hair.

For those few weeks until the hair returns, this woman can enjoy the relative invisibility of a 'normal' female appearance.

The idea of acceptance inherent in the notion of performance hovers somewhere between Bourdieu's insistence on the alignment between the habitus and the social structure, and Butler's more fluid sense of performativity. For Bourdieu (1984, 1990), the attainment of a social identity is the result of practice, the operation of the habitus and the sedimentation of these processes in the body. The development of this bodily *hexis* is revealed in speech, deportment and in the operation of taste. In this way the 'choices', if they can properly be called such, leading to receiving treatments in the beauty salon arise as a result of this sedimentation process. Gender identity becomes less of a performance and more the result of position taking by the woman. This position taking is closely aligned to the positioning of the person in the social field (Bourdieu, 1998). Explaining the humble leg wax here becomes an exercise in understanding the gendered habitus and the symbolism of body hair in the dichotomous relationship between male and female. The performance of gender through the use of the beauty salon could be understood in Bourdieu's terms as a form of symbolic capital. Although femininity is not a privileged identity, it can accrue certain benefits in limited spheres, for example, in heterosexual relationships. In this schema the display of taste through consumption and leisure is a means for the woman in a family to convert economic capital into social capital. The woman remains object:

> Bourdieu recognizes women's status as capital-bearing *objects* whose value accrues to the primary groups to which they belong, rather than as capital-accumulating subjects in social space.
>
> (Lovell, 2000, p. 20; emphasis in original)

In contrast, Butler too easily separates sex, gender and sexuality (Butler, 1990). For her there is no necessary and automatic association between sexed bodies, culturally enforced gender codes and sexual desires. Her approach lies between seeing gender as a noun representing a pre-existing entity, and viewing it as a set of free-floating attributes. Gender is an achievement, and one which is never complete or finished, but one which requires constant performance and reiteration for its existence. This potentiality is constrained by gender itself and anything which does not conform to our understanding of the established gender order is unthinkable. The value of the abject, or the 'outside' of these gender norms, is that they establish the coherence and intelligibility of the inside. However, Butler does allow for acts which transgress the established gender order, and it is perhaps here that her interest lies. Performativity in this sense allows for resistance in the form of the playful, the ironic or the subversive. It is in this area that Butler has been accused of voluntarism in allowing for these transgressive performances, a charge which she has strenuously denied (Butler, 1993).

A return to Skeggs is useful here (Skeggs, 1997). Despite drawing on a schema based around the understanding of capitals closely allied to Bourdieu's work, one of the strengths of her analysis is that she allows for the performative element of femininity to remain ambivalent (Lovell, 2000). She also allows for some degree of resistance. Due to the pathologisation of white working-class womanhood, the women in her study remain ambivalent about their attachment to what Skeggs argues is a bourgeois cultural ideal. The women draw upon and manage their feminine appearance as and when it fits within their own lives. Despite being judged as failures by its standards, they never fully accept those standards. It is Skeggs' acceptance of the woman as subject rather than simply object, and also her fully taking into account the impact of class upon gendered identity, which allows her to understand this ambivalence without resorting to voluntarism on her subjects' part.

Performance forms one part of the three aspects to appropriateness. It is connected to skill and knowledge in that all relate to the being and the doing of gender, and the role of body practices in this process. However, appropriateness also varies according to space. I have already outlined how a sense of biographical time is vital to understanding salon use. In the same way, a sense of social and geographical space is vital to understanding the complex negotiations underpinning appropriateness.

Space

Performance of gender identity varies according to space. Space in this instance refers not only to geographical location but also to social and relational spaces:

> The spatial organization of society . . . is integral to the production of the social, and not merely its result. It is fully implicated in both history and politics.
>
> (Massey, 1994, p. 4)

This understanding of space is both local, national and global and includes a temporal dimension. Within what I have called a space, relationships vary according to others present and the timing of the presence in that space. Reactions of others form an integral characteristic of a particular space, and these others may either be significant to the interviewee in the sense that they are important 'people I know' such as friends and family, or they may be less significant in relational terms but important in other ways (e.g. a boss at work). Timing within the space also varies according to the time of day, to the special events which might be occurring in any particular space (e.g. weddings, important meetings at work, holidays, special social occasions), and also according to the point in the lifecourse.

Connections may be made between the spaces women are able to inhabit and their point in the lifecourse. For example, the movement of girl children may be severely circumscribed by parents and by the society in which they are growing up (Katz and Monk, 1993). Similarly, all male spaces are common in both the social world and social theorising, while the female space is often related to the home. In a globalised environment, however, this distinction is not so easy to maintain (Massey, 1994). One reason beauty salons are so important to women in a vast range of different cultures is that they represent a socially sanctioned meeting space. However, these local spaces are also influenced by the global economic system which encourages the purchase of profitable products and treatments, and presents a normative ideal of femininity.

Spaces which were described by the interviewees as influential on their performance of gender were: work; private space; exercise spaces; the salon; and going out spaces. The salon is in itself an important space but also offers services which facilitate an appropriate bodily being in other social spaces. The salon also offers a feminised space away from external demands upon the woman, and a place where pleasurable attention to the body and the emotions may be obtained.

Work spaces

Work outside of the home is important in that seventeen of the clients interviewed were in full-time employment and all except one student had been in full-time paid work at some time in the past. The nature of the sample dictates that all the beauty therapists were employed at the time of the study. The paid work environment demands of its employees a particular appearance, standards of behaviour and appropriate gender performance, and I will elaborate on the consequences of work-related demands in a later chapter. Work performance varies according to the type of employment, the ethos of the employer and also in relation to contact with the public. The service sector in particular has been at the forefront in regulating the appearance and behaviour expected from its employees (Witz *et al.*, 2003). This has become commonplace to the extent that there are colleges of further education in the UK which require staff to sport name badges and also stipulate the colour of clothes that staff are expected to wear. Name badges are also being considered in at least one UK university. This brings back memories of school days, and I do not look forward to the time when teaching staff are finding ways to undermine the authority of the uniform while faced with students who are relatively freer in their dress code. Women have borne the brunt of this regulation while at the same time receiving fewer of the rewards for adhering to its standards (Adkins and Lury, 1999; Adkins, 2001). This has not gone without comment in popular culture. The TV programme *What Not to Wear*, which I discussed above, devotes much of its time to gaining the reaction of work colleagues to the subject's transformation. The approval of colleagues and bosses is evident when the woman (or more rarely man) who has been nominated for the make-over is presented transformed at the end of the programme. In one case a male employer stated that he was now happier to see the woman concerned as a representative of his company than previously where her dress had been less feminine, and less 'stylish'. All the interviewees in this study were aware of the type of dress and general appearance that was expected of them. This was true of both clients and therapists.

Special occasions such as important presentations or meetings may precipitate a change in dress or a visit to the beauty salon. 'Dealing with the public' at work is also an important influence on how women are expected to perform and to appear in the workplace:

Karen: Some days I don't go [to work] particularly tidy. I don't say I go scruffy but I wouldn't say I looked particularly smart and they don't bat an eyelid. But I think if I stepped out into casual they might say something. If somebody didn't fit the proper image I think they would be very tempted to say. Again I think that would depend on the person and what particular job they had in the organisation.

I: What kinds of jobs would make a difference?

Karen: Well if they are meeting clients all the time then they would expect them to dress the part. OK, I meet bank managers and things like that, and yes I will wear my suit and look the part unless they have called in and I haven't expected them, then they take me as they find me. But I think they try and coach the junior members of staff.

Appropriate femininity, both in the workplace and outside it, is closely policed. All the women were aware of the explicit and implicit sanctions attached to disruptions of the feminised standards of appearance. Clean and tidy were described as minimal requirements. Above this expectations varied. Special occasions within the world of work merited particular attention to appearance and a change in dress. Important meetings or contact with the public were mentioned as situations where dress would be 'smart'. In general, the more contact with the public in employment, the more regulated was the appearance of the worker. Those interviewees who at the time of the interview were self-employed or who had been so in the past discussed this in relation to the way they dressed and presented themselves for work. Fiona mentioned the freedom to set her own standards of appropriateness as one of the attractions of self-employment. She claimed that the routines of a 9-to-5 working life and the standards of office dress would be impossible for her to achieve, and saw both this routine and this way of dressing as representing an ethos she was deliberately rejecting in her work and in her life more generally. In contrast, Mary, who feared that she had lost the necessary skills to produce an acceptable workplace appearance, explained how her visits to the beauty salon were partly as a result of her desire to return to the workplace after an absence due to illness. Advice from beauty therapists was seen as valuable in providing up-to-date information, and in creating an image which restored her own confidence, but also presented the appropriate image to potential employers. I will return to this work space below in discussing the labour of beauty.

Private spaces

Private spaces include the bathroom, or time spent looking in the mirror. It is in these private spaces that women examine themselves intimately for signs of deviations from their own desired body image. Bodies and faces are studied for lines, tone, hair and size. These spaces also provide the woman with the knowledge of her own body which prompts visits to the salon or otherwise. I do not wish to paint a picture here of women overly concerned with external appearance and spending large amounts of time agonising over every perceived imperfection. Time spent in personal spaces can also be affirming, or resignatory. According to other biographical factors this time will be more or less enjoyable and self-critical. Time and ambivalence play an important role here. With age and with changing life circumstances these private moments alter in their meaning and significance. Christina mentioned increased visits to the salon after a boyfriend ended their relationship, at the same time spending more time self-critically examining her appearance in mirrors at home and while out shopping. This phase, however, was short lived. Ambivalence then is a characteristic of these private spaces. None of the women in this study held idealised standards of appearance which they were naively striving towards; rather, all described varying levels of acceptance and pride in their appearance according to time in the lifecourse and other events in their lives. Private spaces allow contemplation of the ambivalent relationship between desire and actuality in the bodily routines of these women. Gender here is a mixture of performativity and self-evaluation.

Exercise spaces

Most common exercise spaces were the gym, the swimming pool and exercise classes. These spaces were present in client narratives either as important places which featured regularly in the woman's life, or in contrast, as spaces that the woman 'should' visit but actually did so rarely or intermittently:

That is a fantasy as well. I keep talking about going to the gym and everyone around me talks about going to a gym, but I've never been to a gym in my life.

(Christina)

For those women who exercised regularly in these formal spaces, not only did exercise form part of a generalised approach to appearance and well-being, but also bodily display during exercise formed one arena for their performance of appropriateness:

The only thing I have done is waxing, usually every few months purely because I don't like shaving and waxing just seems to be a lot better, and also I do a lot of swimming and sports and stuff.

(Karen)

Here the display of the body during sporting activities is presumed to necessitate hair removal. The method of removal is justified, but the fact of its removal is left unquestioned. Similarly, Stephanie described how after leg waxing she wore shorts for her exercise classes but switched to tracksuit bottoms when she felt that her leg hair had reached an unacceptable length.

Going out spaces

Going out is an important social event which constitutes a social space in itself. Going out is an expression of social networks and relationships. The phrase as used by the interviewees includes a variety of very different social occasions which take place in the company of different groups of people ranging from formal dinner receptions held at partners' workplaces with 'people I don't know', through relaxed evenings with a partner or close friend, to 'girls' nights out' in the centre of the city. For each of these types of occasion the performance of appropriateness varies, as does the level of anxiety about this performance. Most nervousness about 'getting it right' is evident during formal occasions with people not known intimately by the interviewee. Such occasions often merit a visit to the salon. In contrast, less performance anxiety is displayed in situations with close friends or a long-standing partner. With new partners, however, a very different type of performance is produced. Christina, who (above) talks of her distress at the end of a relationship, described her actions at the start of that relationship. On early dates with her partner she had worn more make-up than usual. As the relationship continued she decreased both the amount of make-up she wore and the attention paid to preparing for dates. At first she was nervous about spending the night with her partner as he would see her in an unmade-up state. During later stages of their relationship this fear transformed into a symbol of the significance of their intimacy as he had seen her at 'her worst'.

The space entered into demands differing levels of investment in appearance and display. When going out the geography of the city itself is important, since bars, clubs and social venues occasion significant attention to be paid to appearance. It is in these locations that the person feels and expects to be most on view. It is also in these locations that heterosexual women will, within implicit boundaries, expect and welcome comments from men regarding appearance and bodily display:

> When you go out and you are all dressed up and put your make-up on or whatever, its sometimes nice to think that other people find you attractive as well.
>
> (Clare)

Hollands (1995) describes how the social significance of 'going out' has been transformed in the contemporary city. No longer simply a characteristic of a transitional phase between childhood and adulthood, going out has become a more permanent ritual among young adults. This is due to economic restructuring, the increasing role of the city in shaping the lives of young people in particular, and the role of the city in consumption practices (ibid., p. 1). One radical transformation in the contemporary city is the increasing presence of young women, and sometimes in large single-sex groups. This is particularly the case for young white women. The discomfort caused by 'hen parties' claiming physical space, being noisy and freely drinking alcohol is one example of how women have begun to intervene in particular geographical spaces previously closed to them on such terms.[3] In the city of Newcastle in the North of England which Hollands focuses on, the pubs and clubs are divided into areas which are frequented by local people, and those visited by students. Both groups of people are aware of the others' presence but they socialise in very different spaces. The types of bodily display within these areas are also clearly demarcated. Hollands describes vividly how sexuality is vitally important, less in relation to actual sexual encounters, but rather in terms of how 'much of the investment made here [in sexuality] is displaced into clothing, posture, innuendo and conversation' (ibid., p. 58).

Display, and particularly the display of sexuality and sexual availability or otherwise, are displaced into appearance, and again it is here that the beauty industry enters to provide the professional advice and services required to manage this display. This is particularly the case for heterosexual women, but is also increasingly true for heterosexual and gay men. The evidence in this study for lesbians' use of beauty salons is more ambiguous and anecdotal. All interviewees reported themselves to be heterosexual and no mention was made by therapists of lesbian clients.

The preparation for 'nights on the town' may become a social event in itself where dressing and applying make-up form part of the social rituals of friendship between groups of women (O'Neill, 1993; Skeggs, 1997). Preparation for going out and the evaluation of what is appropriate then vary according to the geographical location of the social event, those who are present during the occasion, and the level of formality.

Most anxiety is generated in unfamiliar situations or with unknown people where the rules of social engagement are less a part of the familiar routines of life. Here there is much more scope for unknowingly transgressing some implicit rule which would show the woman up as being out of place. This anxiety relates both to the performance of gender and of class. It is possible to 'give away' a class background through accent, dress or manners.

The now mythical question, 'Does my bum look big in this?' is an illustration of how women may feel that their bodies are always and everywhere 'out of place'.

The services of the beauty therapist in offering advice on appropriateness and in achieving it are most often called upon where the woman is unsure of the etiquette of the situation, such as during rare formal dinners, or in preparation for special events where the client wishes to display the fact that she recognises the significance of the event by 'making an effort'. Good examples of this type of 'going out' are weddings. The services of a beauty therapist are called on to facilitate a bodily display reflecting social relationships. The recognition of the significance of a wedding is displayed by the care taken with appearance. The external validation and expertise of a worker in the beauty industry who is perhaps more able to translate the 'rules' of appearance reassure the woman that she is less likely to transgress or to be 'exposed'. Here then the beauty therapist is contributing to maximising the bodily capital of the client in a form which will be recognised in that particular space, but also more generally.

The salon

Finally, the salon itself forms a separate space, entry to which the client prepares herself for, in one case by claiming, 'I always put on my whitest bra and my best knickers'. In the salon the client receives advice and treatment which feed back into her knowledge, skill and performance of gender identity. It is generally a space within which the client feels separated from her everyday life and within it she may experience 'time for herself' and 'time in the salon' in the ways I have described above. The reason clients visit salons and the treatments they receive vary, but a common experience is that the salon represents a space apart from the routines of everyday life. The phrase 'like a mini holiday' used by one client to describe time in the salon points to the liminality of the salon operating as a space somewhere between 'home' and 'holiday' (Shields, 1990). However, this is most true in relation to pampering treatments. For those clients who receive regular grooming or corrective treatments such as electrolysis or waxing, the salon is much less a place of escape and much more a functional space.

The clients interviewed searched for their preferred salon, often attending for a small treatment in order to test out the service offered before committing to more involved and expensive treatments. In the UK, rather than complain if a treatment is unsatisfactory or if the client does not feel that she has received an adequate service, it seems that the woman is more likely to search out a salon where the experience does live up to her expectations. If the client does not feel comfortable in the salon space then she will take her custom elsewhere. The means by which this comfort is established are related to the segmented nature of beauty salons. In aiming their décor, services and prices at niche markets, the business of the salon is carefully targeted at customers in terms of ethnicity, class, age and gender. In fact every study of a beauty salon with which I am familiar illustrates the relative homogeneity of the clientele and the effect this has on social relationships formed inside (see e.g. Furman, 1997; Rooks, 1998; Willett, 2000; Gimlin, 2002). The clients recognise these symbols in salons, as do the therapists:

> Maybe the smaller unregistered type salons that really couldn't give a damn, maybe it fulfils a place in the market place for those that don't want to pay more for better qualified, well turned out therapists who know what they're talking about. Maybe some people just want like the hairdressers that are on the corner of the street 'Oh I go there because it's handy', you know. OK your perm looks a total pig's ear and you didn't come out with the right colour on your hair, but it hasn't cost them much and it'll soon grow out. Perhaps it's the same sort of thing in beauty.
>
> (Colette BT)

Colette is clearly referring to the social class of clientele. This is indicated by several cues in the text. The terms 'pay more', 'better qualified' and 'better turned out' refer to the economic capital available to the client but also to the indicators of educational and cultural capital on the part of therapists. 'On the corner of the street' locates the salon in a specific geographical location. As housing in both Europe and North America is most often segmented, establishing that the salon is on the street corner assures its homogenised and local clientele. In the UK the decline in the popularity of the 'perm' as a hairstyle has allowed the identification of those who still 'perm' their hair as working class. Salons then are not neutral spaces but highly segmented. The woman searches for a space where she feels at ease, and where she feels her particular tastes will be catered for.

Rachel described her preparations for a visit to the salon. In doing so she clearly outlines the differentiation between salons and their clientele:

Rachel: I would rather stick to more local salons. I don't know whether this is peculiar to me or whether that is a class issue or what, but there is this image of maybe posh women with long nails and Mercedes and Prada handbags and I don't think I can compete with that, although I have got a designer handbag which I always take.

I: You always take it with you?

Rachel: Of course I do and I always take my mobile and wear my Gucci glasses.

For Rachel the experience of salon use was partly one of inadequacy and discomfort. Her politicised critique of the beauty industry weighed heavily against her visits to beauty salons. However, this was an unusual example. In most cases the salon is seen as a safe and relaxing space in that clients have self-screened and are present in any particular location only if their sense of 'ease' is confirmed.

The therapists describe their salons as a feminised space and clients mentioned that they did not like the presence of men in the salon:

I think it offers a female retreat, even though we are getting into that male market, but I still think the female client
wants to get away from those men. And it is a very female
orientated place.

(Sue BT)

Male presence resulted in fears about display of the body and of
standards of appearance which were less of a concern in an all-
female environment. In contrast, some women selected a salon
because of its perceived gender neutrality in terms of décor and
ambience. On closer inspection this avoidance of the outward symbols of femininity such as 'girly' décor and pastel shades actually
combines with it a critique of a particular type of working-class
femininity. In rejecting the taste displayed by pink uniforms and
chintz curtains, the clients are making a statement about their
comfort with a specific form of middle-class femininity (Skeggs,
2001). To prefer the round rooms, deep colours, fresh-brewed
coffee and leather armchairs is as much about consuming an
image of a segment of the middle class targeted by the multinational
beauty companies as it is about enticing male clients into the salon.

Empty spaces

One of the key spaces which is missing from the testimonies of the
interviewees is the space of the 'bedroom' or spaces which relate to
sexuality. In fact only Suki ever mentioned sex explicitly during the
interviews. At the end of each interview every woman was given a
chance to ask me questions or to make any additional comments.
Suki replies:

Suki: I'm pleased that you didn't ask anything about sex really.
     I thought you might.
I: Why, did you think there might be a connection?
Suki: It wasn't me actually, it was my husband. He said, 'well she
     might ask you if feeling good is related to your sex life and you
     might wander down that avenue'. I said, 'Well I haven't actually
     but I shall be aware if it comes up'.

Here the connection is made between her own feelings about her body and the effect this has on the sexual relationship with her partner. Interestingly, it is the male partner who raises this connection and who appears to be uneasy about the interview in case this area is discussed. This unease and my own lack of direct questioning may contribute to the fact that sexual spaces are missing from the discussion. However, sexuality may more accurately be described as an absent presence. Questions of sexuality are wider than references simply to sexual activity. In the background of all of the interviews with therapists and clients, and tangible during my time in salons, was reference to normative heterosexuality. Heterosexuality operates as a default position, presumed and uncommented upon. Only when discussing male clients in the salon, or the treatments accessed by male-to-female transsexuals, was the all-encompassing heterosexuality of the salon ever breached. In these cases men were assumed to be gay with two possible scenarios which might reinstate their heterosexuality. Only if they were presumed to be 'businessmen' attending the salon for 'grooming', or if their female partner made the appointment for them or was visibly present in the salon, were men regarded as unquestionably heterosexual. I am aware that this is partly dependent upon the sampling underpinning the empirical data presented here. In fact in one of the cities where fieldwork was conducted, a salon aimed at men, located in an area catering to gay men, was opened. Attempts to gain access to this salon for research purposes were brought to an end by the closing down of the enterprise in a short space of time. In the vast majority of salons, and among the majority of women clients, heterosexuality is presumed and therefore not commented upon.

Getting in and getting it right: some concluding comments

Salon use is varied. It varies according to the client and her biographical specificity, and with the types and volume of treatments accessed. In order to initiate salon visits potential clients must feel that treatments there fit with their worldview and their self-view. They must then find the time, money and justificatory tools to begin their visits. The variety of treatments, salons and clients means that attempting to understand this process is an exercise in seeing patterns in shifting stories. In order to do this I have interwoven evidence from client and therapist interviews with theoretical approaches which, I believe, are the most convincing. In doing so I have broken down salon use into 'getting in', and 'getting it right'. The impetus to getting in is the interplay between self-view, worldview and time. The key to understanding one of the primary roles of the salon is my concept of appropriateness.

One of the criticisms of appropriateness could be that it over-emphasises conformity. In Bourdieu's terms femininity can be little other than complicit. However, I hope that by using appropriateness we can see that complicity is not total and spaces for ambivalence remain. In terms of beauty salon use I also argue that we should not fall into the trap of viewing all engagement with the beauty industry as wholly negative and complicit. Escape from external demands into the feminised world of the salon can allow for recuperation and the forming of social bonds between women. The segmentation of salons also allows these relationships to facilitate support within ethnic and class groups. The pure sensuality of some treatments is also not to be dismissed, and would probably be treated with more respect if it occurred in the context of complementary therapies. I have also attempted to understand the operation of a gendered hierarchy of power through the body. Power here marks the body through objective social structures and subjective processes of feeling, emotion and desire. Despite this fact, the clients in this study were all highly sceptical of the operations of the beauty industry. All worked hard to reconcile their own use of its services with this scepticism. Conformity in most of these women's lives was accompanied by the seductive pleasures of the beauty salon *and* the critical rejection of its claims.

Notes

1 Although this is generally the case, it should also be noted that a significant proportion of economically advantaged women in the USA in particular employ domestic workers to perform household tasks for them. This places a further burden on poor women, and women from ethnic minorities (Ehrenreich and Hochschild, 2003).

2 Ann Summers is an organisation which sells 'sex toys', lingerie, erotic fiction and other sex-related products in a string of stores in the UK. The company also employs women to organise parties in the homes of interested individuals in order to allow home shopping. These parties have gained a certain notoriety as places where women engage in sex-related games and explicit conversations about sex.

3 Hen parties are the celebrations undertaken by women prior to marriage. The male equivalent is the 'stag party'. In the UK both social occasions involve the careful separation of the sexes. It is also common to wear fancy dress and to consume large quantities of alcohol. Certain locations in the UK have become popular for hen parties, and have begun to aim their tourist trade towards them.

Chapter 4

The hidden labour of beauty

I don't know whether this sounds a very sexist thing to say but in reality it's an extremely good career for a woman. I think it's ideal for women because we utilise all those intuitive skills that we have and that we do, so I think its ideal.

(Amanda BT)

The term 'beauty therapy' suggests a conjunction of ideas incorporating a transformation involving mind, body or both. Both beauty and therapy also contain the implicit assumption of labour – the labour of the body and the creation of a sense of self for both the therapist and client. It is useful to examine the consequences of the claims of both beauty work and therapy for the professional status and working life of therapists. In particular I will examine the role that 'emotional labour' (Hochschild, 1983), 'aesthetic labour' (Witz *et al.*, 2003) or 'body work' (Tyler and Hancock, 2001) play in their work. I will also examine the role of particular types of treatments, specifically those which I have described as 'grooming', in the working lives of beauty salon clients, and link these treatments to a postulated aestheticisation of the workplace (Adkins and Lury, 1999, 2000; Adkins, 2001).

The work of the beauty therapist

Beauty therapy encompasses a diverse and wide range of treatments carried out in a number of different locations. The therapist may choose to specialise in massage, manicures or hair removal:

> I happened to excell at electrolysis which I love. And its weird isn't it the twists and turn that life takes you? I mean, it was a career that I didn't even know existed. Its quite a bizarre thing when you think of people spending their day just removing hair, but strangely enough I just love it.
>
> (Yvette BT)

Alternatively she may remain a generalist, particularly in smaller salons, where she must be capable of delivering all services offered in that establishment, although this route through the profession appears to be declining as the number and types of treatments increase:

> The thing that has altered is we used to be beauty therapists and do everything and now because it's such a wide range of treatments you tend to find that people are specialising. So, they're becoming either a beautician that works within a hair salon and does make-up, nails, eyelashes, eyebrows, facials, waxing, or they're becoming a salon therapist which is beauty, body, electrolysis, or they're becoming a massage therapist workng with a health spa, gymnasium, health hydro, that type of situation, or specialising as a nail technician, because nails are taking off now enormously, or specialising in hair removal and waxing, sugaring, threading, electrolysis, which I think is good because obviously if you're specialising then you actually become better at those treatments.
>
> (Emily BT)

There is a tense debate within the industry about the relative importance of the 'beauty' side of their work compared to

'therapy'. This debate reflects the relative specialisms of the therapists. Some argue that 'beauty' should be dropped from the title
of the profession in order to raise professional status and to
emphasise the types of treatments carried out which have little to
do with appearance. Others argue that their financial security
rests on the 'bread and butter' beauty treatments.

Beauty therapy at present does not constitute a unified professional or occupational group. There is a no single professional
body with which all beauty therapists must register in order to lay
claim to the title of beauty therapist. In the UK there is a diversity
of nationally recognised training programmes delivered mainly
through colleges of further education. There are also many private
colleges offering their own diplomas, and commercial companies
which manufacture cosmetics and therapeutic equipment often
provide courses of training in their use. None the less, the beauty
therapists interviewed seemed to have a relatively coherent sense
of their collective identity, though with little sense of a well-
defined collective 'professional project' . All interviewees defined
beauty therapy in terms of work with *feelings* as well as with the
body. Beauty therapy is a professional occupation at the same time
as remaining a service industry. Beauty treatments are also driven
by the logic of profit. The professional expertise and status of the
therapist lie between the medical professional, the complementary
therapist and the sex worker.

Learning to be a beauty therapist

> Whatever you do, you do to meet the needs of the business.
> (Kerry BT)

A career in beauty therapy in the UK entails work placements
during training for which pay is minimal. Upon completing a
three-year course of training the therapist finds work either in a
large salon or a smaller high street salon. She works as a junior,
slowly building up her own clientele. Sometimes she may 'go
mobile' if she believes that she has a significant client base.

In order to progress, continuous training is required in new techniques, new products, and specialist areas such as aromatherapy or reflexology. The drop-out rate from the profession is significant at this stage. A combination of low pay, long hours and disillusionment with the profession are the impetus for this exodus. In the long term, beauty therapists aim to own their own salon. In this way the beauty salon is a significant source of female self-employment.

> I think we train really hard and we work really hard and we don't get recognised for it whatsoever, and I think that especially in the larger companies the employers know this and they take advantage of it. In the salon where I work . . . we actually work nine hours per day and they pay us for eight, so there's an hour they don't actually pay us for that we're entitled to. . . . And they say well, get a sandwich when you've got five minutes between clients. I mean I've gone from 9 till 4 without anything to eat and there's nothing you can do about it because the government don't recognise us as being a professional. They don't offer any support at all whereas if you worked in a bank and you had to work from 9 till 4, all hell would break loose, whereas in a salon it's perfectly OK to work you like slaves, pay you a pittance and get away with it.
>
> (Louise BT)

This young woman went on to recount how when she first began working in a salon she worked for forty-five hours per week for £100, and that, four years later at the time of her interview in 1998, she was earning little more. She also described a succession of managers in her salon, the first of which was paid £360 per week, the following manager, £260, the next £240. Therapists were expected to generate three times their wages in till receipts for twelve consecutive weeks before they were allowed a pay rise. This is borne out by the fact that the pay for beauty therapists in the UK from 2000 to 2002 remained static. In fact, in 2002 figures actually fell back a little. In 2000 the average hourly pay for a therapist was £4.93, for a senior therapist £6.31 and for a salon manager £8.63. In 2002 these respective figures stood at £4.88, £6.18, and £6.86. Nail technicians received £3.89, a surprising figure, since this is actually below the legal minimum wage (Guild News, 2002).

Louise also told of therapists in salons, particularly in large department stores, who had contracted bladder and bowel infections through not being allowed to go to the toilet during the day. The therapist is not allowed to leave a client waiting, and where appointments are booked one after the other there is no time allowed for toilet or meal breaks. These conditions are not common to all salons, and often in the small businesses therapists may receive more favourable employment conditions. However, long hours and low pay are endemic in the industry. Despite being subject to laws concerning health and safety, and workers' rights, the industry is poorly regulated and generally non-unionised, which contributes to these abuses of employment standards.

The professional status of the beauty therapist

> You can't be pretty and brainy. You are either one or the other.
>
> (Wendy BT)

The professional status of the beauty therapist is an ongoing and sensitive issue for the industry. Defining what constitutes a profession is difficult and open to debate. For example, an interpretive approach might regard a profession as 'an ascribed symbolic, socially negotiated status based day to day interaction' (Allsop and Saks, 2002, p. 5). A Foucauldian approach in contrast emphasises discursive formations which underpin the claims to professional status. An increasingly dominant neo-Weberian definition argues that professions are:

> Special kinds of knowledge-based occupations. The type of knowledge, the social and cultural value attributed to it and the way in which each occupation handles that knowledge

are seen as central to both the process of professionalization and maintaining/extending professional positions.

(Allsop and Saks, 2002, p. 4)

Witz (1992) has criticised these definitions for imposing a neutral and essentialised approach which fails to take into account the gendered nature of professions and the struggles over power inherent in this gendered system. The material generated during the course of this research does not allow for a full investigation of beauty therapy's professionalising project. My more limited objective here is to understand how the beauty therapists in this study viewed their own professional role.

The beauty therapists did not show a great deal of involvement with professional organisations. All except three belonged to one or other of the organisations claiming to represent beauty therapists, but most claimed to have joined primarily for the insurance cover offered. Many justified this low level of involvement through sceptical remarks about the organisations (as run by a set of 'prima donnas', as 'cliquey' or undemocratic, as run by a bunch of 'crusty middle-aged ladies with blue rinses'). But perhaps the main problem in the interviewees' eyes was the feeling that the professional associations did not have much power to address the issues of standards and public esteem. They were seen as having much less clout than either the official accreditation bodies or the powerful commercial companies. In this respect they were very unlike other professional groups who have sought to legitimate their expertise and status. For example, the complementary therapists in Cant and Sharma's study were often very critical of the professional organisations they belonged to, but saw their role as crucial in the struggle for security and public esteem, and tended to identify strongly with the 'professional projects' pursued by the organisations even if they did not always agree with their specific actions (Cant and Calnan, 1991; Sharma, 1995, p. 161).

There was general agreement that low pay and status was a major problem for beauty therapists as a group. Most of the interviewees felt that beauty therapy was a profession or ought to be regarded as such (only one therapist felt that it was really no more than a service industry). They gave two main justifications for this view. First, they argued that beauty therapy involves complex knowledge of the human body, perhaps comparable to that of a nurse. A second argument was that a beauty therapist is 'professional' in her dealings with clients. She must merit the client's trust, yet also maintain a businesslike detachment, be responsive but not over-involved. Yet there was a feeling that the beauty therapists' work was generally undervalued and trivialised.

Individual therapists and the wider industry have a hard time in shaking off the 'bimbo' image, or presumptions about lack of training. The beauty therapists were aware of their image as 'bimbo':

> We have all had to deal with the 'oh they just paint nails and do massage . . . nudge, nudge, wink, wink'. Men tend to regard it kind of smuttily, and women sometimes, perhaps they have never had a beauty treatment, women tend to think we are all brainless bimbos. They see you as superficial, frivolous, not terribly intelligent. And men just think it's massage [laughs].
>
> (Amanda BT)

Often beauty therapists are confused with beauticians, the women behind beauty counters in large stores who give advice on make-up and beauty products. This confusion caused much annoyance. The beauty therapists see themselves as highly qualified, specialist professionals. Their training includes knowledge of human biology, information on the use of chemicals and any contra-indications which may occur, some level of business knowledge and accounting, and so on. They are keen to point this out and to emphasise that they are not simply 'the girls who couldn't hack it at school'. Those therapists who had been trained several years previously had received a Higher National Diploma (HND) qualification which was seen as highly theoretical, and highly prized, gaining favourable comparison not only to nursing qualifications, but also to university-based degree-level qualifications.

In more recent years, training has moved towards National Vocational Qualifications (NVQs), and all but one of the beauty therapists saw this as a decline in standards. In the NVQ, assessment is continuous, and the emphasis is placed upon practical as well as theoretical knowledge. Interestingly, the therapist who saw NVQs as an improvement was the proprietor of a salon frequented primarily by a white working-class clientele, and also one who was emphatically not interested in more holistic or complementary therapies.

Another unfavourable comparison is made with hairdressers where a certain amount of rivalry exists. Again, hairdressers are seen as less qualified, due partly to their own NVQ qualification structure, and somehow less professional. In the UK the work environment of hairdressers is seen to encourage this unprofessionalism, since clients are treated in a communal room where conversations can be overheard. In contrast, the beauty therapist prides herself on her attention to the individual needs of the client and the maintenance of discretion at all times, both of which are fostered by the provision of private treatment rooms. This is in direct contrast to salons in the USA where the communal treatment of clients is part of the social experience of visiting the salon (Furman, 1997; Rooks, 1998). Nail salons in the UK offer communal treatment areas, so facilitating social exchange between clients as well as between therapist and client. This may be one reason for the growth in popularity of such enterprises as the visit to the nail salon becomes a shared leisure activity. However, beauty therapists are often dismissive of the nail technicians who run these businesses as they do not have to be formally qualified in the way that professional beauty therapists must.

The beauty therapists were ambivalent about telling people outside of other professionals and clients about their work. At social occasions many mentioned that they did not discuss their occupation. For those teaching beauty therapy it was easily disguised by calling themselves lecturers. However, this does not mean that the therapists themselves are not proud of their craft, and having to disguise their profession to avoid negative comment caused much resentment.

Wendy: If you tell people [that you are a beauty therapist], especially when you are out, and you might get talking to a member of the opposite sex and they say, 'What do you do for a living?' I lie.

I: Why don't you want to tell them?

Wendy: Because I just think they will think, 'Oh she is really into massage', 'Oh but we knew that, you can tell'. And I just don't want to listen to all of the ridiculous comments, so I just tell them I am a receptionist in a hotel.

As Wendy explains, a further implicit assumption around beauty therapy is the perceived sexualised nature of the therapist's work. For some 'outsiders', the massage in the beauty salon and that in the massage parlour may have similar connotations. The therapist wishes to be taken seriously as a professional and so must not only avoid the bimbo label, but also the perceived overlap with the role of the sex worker. One of the reasons for this presumption is that in addition to a significant amount of intimate work with the body, beauty therapy is an occupation which may be characterised as involving a high degree of what has been termed 'emotional labour' (Hochschild, 1983).

Understanding emotional labour

It's good discipline for me that I have to be nice to people all the time [laughs], because I mean we wouldn't through choice would we? I think at the end of the day it had the effect that I didn't really want to go out and socialise with new people because I had to do it all day. . . . I like meeting people. I didn't like meeting everybody that I met in there [salon].

(Zoe BT)

Hochschild's publication *The Managed Heart* (1983) has provoked a wide-ranging debate on the nature of emotional management within the workplace and specifically in the service sector. More recently a variety of concepts have been added to examine the somaticised work of the (usually female) service worker (see, for example, 'aesthetic labour' – Witz *et al.*, 2003; 'body work' – Tyler and Hancock, 2001). I will draw on some of these arguments to frame the following discussion of the role of corporeal and emotional labour in the work of beauty therapists.

In her study of flight attendants, supplemented by a small study of bill collectors, Hochschild argues that not only the physical labour and time of the employee are demanded by her employer, but also that the management and display of emotions has become an integral requirement of service sector work. In fact the subtitle of the book is 'The commercialization of human feeling'. In this discussion she makes a distinction between emotional labour and emotion work:

> I use the term emotional labour to mean management of feeling to create a publicly observable facial and bodily display; emotional labour is sold for a wage and therefore has an *exchange value*. I use the synonymous terms *emotion work* or *emotion management* to refer to these same acts done in a private context where they have *use value*.
>
> (Hochschild, 1983, p. 7; italics in original)

In contrast, other writers have focused upon the moulding of the physicality of workers in contemporary organisations. Also examining the work of the flight attendant, Tyler and Hancock (2001) argue that:

> The essentialised female body is required to act as the material signifier of an organizational (service) ethos, and it is managed through highly gendered techniques of corporeal management, demanding skilled labour or 'body work', which is effectively naturalized (and therefore not remunerated) because it is performed by women.
>
> (Tyler and Hancock, 2001, p. 26)

Through a process of 'incorporation', the female flight attendant learns how to give off bodily signals which will relax the nervous passenger. She also receives detailed instructions about the management of her appearance, in contrast to male flight attendants who are simply required to 'look clean and "socially attractive"' (p. 33). This regulation of the body even extends to weighing the woman flight attendant to ensure that she maintains a strict weight–height ratio (Tyler and Abbott, 1998). Despite the level of skill and effort which goes into such body management, the woman worker is not rewarded for her efforts. Working on the body is seen as a leisure activity for women, and the skills required as immanent feminine characteristics rather than learned social skills.

Similarly, Witz *et al.* argue that aesthetic labour has become fundamental to the contemporary service industries. Following Bourdieu (1984), they define aesthetic labour as: 'The mobilization, development and commodification of embodied "dispositions"' (Witz *et al.*, 2003, p. 37). Their point here is that workers enter the labour market with capacities and skills but that these are seen increasingly as part of the raw material moulded and commodified by industries in pursuit of both profit and the promotion of their company image. The worker becomes the embodiment of company ethos:

> Employers then mobilize, develop and commodify these embodied dispositions through processes of recruitment, selection and training, *transforming* them into 'skills' which are geared toward producing a 'style' of service encounter that appeals to the senses of the customer.
>
> (ibid., italics in original)

The shift here is from Hochschild's emphasis upon the transformation of feeling through the management process to viewing modes of embodiment as equally transformed in contemporary employment practices. By drawing on Bourdieu, Witz *et al.* are able to show how modes of embodiment are not simply about appearances, but rather, as signifiers of physical capital, they indicate the habitus and social position of the bearer. Although these schemes of bodily being are not fixed once and for all, they are clear indications of past and present position in a field of social relations. However, as they point out, Bourdieu is concerned primarily with class reproduction and focuses his discussion at the societal level; as such his work requires interpretation if it is to be applied in different contexts. What these writers do is to apply Bourdieu, along with a 'rehabilitated' reading of Goffman (1959, 1967, 1971; cited in Witz *et al.*, 2003, p. 38), to a contemporary workplace in order to provide a case study of aesthetic labour.

The aesthetics *of* organisation are made visible in company 'hardware' such as marketing material and physical spaces. It is here that the ethos of the organisation is expressed through design. Aesthetics *in* organisation relates to the moulding of company employees or 'software' such that behaviour and appearance are associated with 'getting on' at work. The key claim by Witz *et al.* is that this 'hardware' and 'software' have become conflated such that:

> Employees, as software, have become human hardware as they are configured by organizations both as part of the surplus-producing process of the organization and in order to be the *embodiment* of the organization's identity.
>
> (ibid., p. 43)

In their case study of 'Elba Hotels', they show how the corporation recruits and trains staff who are seen as having the potential to embody the Elba ideal. After the 'right' sort of person is selected they are subject to a ten-day induction process where consultants teach grooming and deportment. These sessions include advice on hair, make-up and other standards of appearance. The argument here is that in the new service industries the bodies of workers, rather than simply their emotions, are transformed. Interestingly, Witz *et al.* claim that these processes are now spreading more widely within the employment sector:

> It is our contention that this labour of aesthetics is no longer an occasional initiative of sometimes idiosyncratic or exotic

organizations, or even enterprising individuals, but a deliber-
ate, managerially determined characteristic of an emerging
subsector within services that involve face-to-face, voice-to-
voice interaction between employee and customer.

(ibid., p. 50)

In this sense, Witz *et al.*'s claim is supported by evidence from the
client interviews, since the extent of their contact with the public,
despite differences in employment sector, did appear to influence
the level of somatic regulation.

There is much in both of these arguments which seems per-
suasive. They chime with other work on organisations such as that
of Adkins (2001) who has focused on the gendered nature of performances in the workplace and how these are read and rewarded
according to differentiated criteria. The formation of identity in
and through this labour process is also a central concern, and adds
to Hochschild's contention that emotions are not simply masked
or performed, but rather come to transform the person though
their management. Similarly, in both Witz *et al.*'s work and that
of Adkins, the management of somatic performances at work
serves to *create* the worker and his or her identity, rather than that
identity simply being *recognised*. However, I would question Tyler
and Hancock's assertion that the essentialised *female* body is
required to carry out such a performance. As I shall discuss below
when looking at the role that grooming treatments play in the
work lives of beauty salon clients, it seems more accurate to claim
that it is a specific form of regulated body which is required. One
of the key reasons for the growth in men's use of salons is in
order to produce the 'organisational body' increasingly demanded
of them. In this sense their bodies are becoming increasingly subject to a commodification long associated with women's bodies.
The skills which are produced may therefore be seen as feminised
rather than female *per se*. Indeed, Witz *et al.* make the point that
as aesthetic labour is actually a part of the commodified process of
exchange rather than something somehow beyond it, it is by no
means only female bodies which are subject to commodification.

My key objections to Witz *et al.*'s claims concern the nature of the dispositions which they argue workers arrive with. According to them, 'these embodied dispositions are, we suggest, more flexible than previous discussion has allowed' (p.41). They argue that Elba Hotels looks for the right kind of employee with the correct potentialities, and also that the employee is produced by the company through the ten-day induction process and subsequent management techniques. This selection of the 'correct' type of employee comes across as simply discrimination cloaked in the language of opportunity and potential. So, for example, the age range of applicants is specified and the body size and personal disposition of those interviewed are subject to scrutiny. Surely this is the type of recruitment process which should have been outlawed by equal opportunity legislation years ago? Is this simply a management technique for continuing discriminatory processes? Or rather, are the potential employees self-selecting in that qualifications and preferences for types of employment are matched to the employment applied for? Witz *et al.* do not pursue the implications of their observation concerning the selection of the potential aesthetic labourer, but rather concentrate on the post-employment process of induction.

By claiming that the somatic potentialities of the worker are more flexible than perhaps allowed by Bourdieu, they are to some extent weakening the power of Bourdieu's analysis. The very point of these embodied dispositions is that the social position which they reflect, and the habitus which underpins them, have been established over years and are ingrained into the very fibre of identity and bodies through the bodily hexis (Bourdieu, 1984, 1990). Moving through social space can lead to acute insecurity when the habitus is at odds with the social space in which they find themselves. For example, Lawler (1999) documents beautifully the anxiety and insecurity generated in the lives of women with a working-class background who become middle class. The power here is in showing how although change is possible, this process is by no means without pain. It seems that a ten-day induction process will not fundamentally transform the somatic being of the potential employee. Unless the potentialities preferred in the selection process are already attuned to the type of worker required, it is unlikely that a short period of training could dislodge ways of being so thoroughly ingrained. Does this mean that this analysis may be applied only to a specific sector of the economy, and to a very particular type of worker? If we are to draw on Bourdieu's use of capitals, are a specific set of capitals required in order to gain employment in this aestheticised sector (Bourdieu, 1984)? In particular, is a set of bodily dispositons and a manifestation of the habitus through taste in dress, hairstyle and consumption patterns becoming a 'qualification' for employment?

Bourdieu himself is explicit about the correlation of concern with appearance and the weight it carries in the workplace. Working-class women and those who are not employed outside the home are unlikely to 'conform to the dominant norms of beauty' (Bourdieu, 1984, p. 206). In contrast, it is women of the petit bourgeoisie, who are concentrated in occupations involving 'presentation and representation' (ibid.), who invest in a 'sense of dignity of conduct and correctness of manners' (ibid.). If this is the case then further questions need to be asked about the class background and the ethnicity of such employees – i.e. who possesses and who does not possess the capitals necessary for service employment, and how easily, if at all, they may be acquired. If they are to be acquired, what role does the beauty industry itself play in this acquisition? In attempting to disentangle the arguments around emotional labour/aesthetic labour I will now explore the dual case study of the work of the beauty therapist and the role of grooming treatments in the working lives of salon clients.

Emotional labour in the work of the beauty therapist

If you're the sort of person that goes into beauty therapy you're a giver, or you should be a giver. Beauty therapists are givers, they're not takers. A good beauty therapist wants that person to feel better when they leave. It's not a question of 'right, I've done that, off the bed, give me the money'.

> A good beauty therapist isn't like that. A good beauty therapist, the greatest reward for her is when a woman comes out and she's smiling, it really is the greatest reward.
>
> (Wendy BT)

Which elements of beauty therapy may be said to involve emotional or aesthetic labour, and are these useful terms to help us to understand the work of beauty therapists? The beauty therapy industry is fragmented, yet when the therapists in this study were asked whether there was any generic service which beauty therapy delivered, there was unanimous reference to *feelings*:

I: Is there anything that makes beauty therapy *one* thing, more than a collection of different specialisms?

Amanda (BT):   We are all trying to make people feel better. That is the common thing, I think, really, making people feel better, giving people confidence.

This theme was raised and elaborated time and again:

> It gives [clients] a better feeling, they feel better and it's introducing things they might not have thought of. Once you have, they feel better so they have benefited from it. They say that God loves you if you love yourself. You have to give happiness to other people, don't you?
>
> (Nathalie BT)

Beauty therapists did not deny the fact that treatments effect real transformations in appearance, nor did they play down the technical expertise needed to use products and equipment (although they might be sceptical about the commercial claims of some products and treatments). But the generic product which the labour of the beauty therapist created was described as *subjective*:

> You make them look nice. I think you give them a feeling of well-being, I think they get that attention for that period

of time which perhaps they don't get in other areas of their lives.

(Gillian BT)

Relations with clients

Therapists experience an ambivalent relationship with clients encompassing the role of the trained professional offering advice, and also the service worker being paid to give the client what she wants. In addition, the beauty therapists in this study also claimed a counselling role in their work where they perform the function of an intimate yet detached listener. Despite the range of treatments available in the salon all are delivered in the context of attentiveness to the client's individual needs and circumstances:

> When a client comes in you'll say, 'Oh, how did your son's wedding go, how did the party go, did you enjoy that night out, was the film good?' And I think that makes them feel . . . interesting. Because we all want to feel that as well, we want to feel loved and interesting. And I think [beauty therapists] do that.
>
> (Amanda BT)

This care and consideration is also delivered in a style which is unique to the individual therapist, consistent with her own personality. The product of beauty therapy is not standardised:

> You get clients who are sort of *your* clients . . . it is very much on an individual client basis, I would say.
>
> (Yvette BT)

A beauty therapist makes herself valuable to the salon by building up such a personal clientele, although there is always the danger that if she leaves to work elsewhere her clientele will follow her. To make the client feel that she is getting total and individual attention, the therapist must work on her relationship with the client and this involves working on her own emotions. For instance, she must gauge the extent to which the client wants to talk during treatment, and what subjects she wants to talk about. During a facial or massage:

> You've got to know when to talk and when to keep your gob shut 'cos you know that if they're going to relax they're not going to want to talk about where they are going for their weekend or where they went on holiday, so you've got to change.
>
> (Janet BT)

Conversation needs to be controlled, and the therapist must not be drawn into discussion of controversial topics or raise them herself. This avoidance of sensitive areas forms one of the basic claims to professional ethics:

> We have, like, these rules. You don't talk about religion, you don't talk about sex, you don't talk about politics, you've got to know your key things that you do not discuss. But then you've still got to be quite relaxed with that client, not just talk about beauty therapy and be all regimental, you've got to show that you're a human being as well, and that if they want to talk about anything then, you know, you are there to listen.
>
> (Janet BT)

The relaxing atmosphere of the salon often encourages confidences and intimacy which the therapist might not always find easy to handle. Or she might simply have to control her irritation:

> You do have clients who will treat you like a waitress. 'Do you really find it nice, filing nails all day long, do you like doing manicures'? . . . The comments that come out! 'I could never sit and wax, it would bore me.' Well it bores me too but you can't tell the client that, you know, you've got to grin and bear it.
>
> (Kirsty BT)

Sometimes this control is difficult to achieve, especially for the inexperienced beauty therapist. The need to respond to the client emotionally without stirring up inappropriate feelings can lead to a dilemma in that her listening role and the light and compliant touch with which the beauty therapist must treat the 'relaxed client' can make it difficult for her to speak out if she thinks the client's choice of treatment or use of products is unwise. She is not in a powerful position to assert a professional opinion. As Diane says:

> When she [client] turns round and says, 'Your cream's not working', I might want to say, 'Yes, in my professional opinion it is, but you're not using it properly, that's where we have got a difference.' It is a very hard industry because it's professional plus service, it's really hard to wear both caps.
>
> (Diane BT)

Here is a potential dilemma for the worker at the front line of the beauty industry, which applies to hairdressing as well:

> By providing for their clients emotionally, beauticians *both* support and undermine their own identity claims. On one hand, by becoming their customers' confidantes and advisers, hairdressers are able to imagine themselves their clients' friends and, by implication, their equals. And seeing themselves as filling the same purpose as therapists, stylists could again find support for their claims to professional status. At the same time, however, because the beauticians imagine themselves their clients' self sacrificing, devoted friends, they are forced to put their patrons' hair styling wishes before their own.
>
> (Gimlin, 1996, pp. 524–5)

The very 'professionalism' that demands self-control and deference to the client's mood and wishes can inhibit the confident expression of authoritative professional knowledge.

Training for emotional labour

While the beauty therapists compared themselves to counsellors, psychiatrists, nurses or psychotherapists with respect to the way they addressed clients' subjective needs, they had difficulty in identifying the sources of these interpersonal skills. Most interviewees felt that they were acquired through ordinary experience rather than through explicit professional training. One therapist explained the response to the client's emotional needs as something you just 'picked up':

> I don't know . . . you just pick it up because you're reading the signals the clients are giving you. So if you didn't know it when you first went into the salon. . . you'd certainly pick it up off the clients, from their body language and from what they're telling you.
>
> (Julie BT)

Julie presents her own personality as her main resource:

> The way I am with the clients is *me* personally. It's not . . . I've got the basics from here [college], what not to talk about, but the way I am with my clients is just me. It's not anything I've been shown how to do or shown how to be, it just comes from experience.
>
> (Julie BT)

Limited life experience was regarded as a problem for the young newly qualified beauty therapist. One interviewee deplored the competence-based approach of NVQs in these terms:

> You see, with NVQs there are 16-year-old girls coming in, they've no skills at all, no life skills, they'll just be wanting to talk about their latest boyfriend, what they did down the local club. What are the clients getting out of that?
>
> (Colette BT)

Another recalled how unprepared she felt when she first started work as a beauty therapist some years ago, implying that this problem was not new:

> I think there is a great gap in the training, that they don't pre-
> pare you. I mean when I went to college I was 20 and I was
> quite naive and I had women confiding in me their innermost
> secrets that they wouldn't tell their best friend about . . . I was
> never prepared for that. But I would listen. A lot of the teen-
> agers I see, they just haven't got what it takes.
>
> (Sue BT)

Another therapist referred to a unit which she taught called 'relationships with clients', but felt that:

> Putting it on paper and doing it in theory, and being in a situa-
> tion are quite different . . . quite different.
>
> (Gillian BT)

This did not mean that the teachers of beauty therapy interviewed felt that they did nothing at all to prepare the student
for the emotional work she would have to do in the salon. But
on the whole they suggested that this preparation was mostly
delivered implicitly in the course of technical training, i.e. not as
a separate topic:

> I mean some of it is verbal, but a lot of it it's like, erm . . . you
> know, it's the unwritten rule. . . . You pick it up as you go
> along. [Tutors] tell you what would you do in this situation,
> how would you handle this? You pick a lot of it up when
> you get into the practical side of things. . . . Situations arise
> in practical sessions in salons like that, you know, which
> [students] come to the tutor with, and they offer a solution
> and they'll learn from it.
>
> (Gillian BT)

Another college therapist reflected that this kind of learning came from a combination of experience and the student's own personality; a few students were only ever interested in the technical side of the therapy and would never make sensitive therapists. A few had a gift for relating to people from the start. For the majority it was a combination of reflective practice and personal maturation. There was therefore a potential contradiction between their claim that beauty therapy involves a high degree of transmitted skills and theoretical knowledge (and that therefore therapists deserve more serious respect than they get) and their failure to locate what they themselves identified as key skills in formal training processes.

Emotional labourer – not sex worker

The therapists, by their own account, are expected to deliver services requiring skills which women either develop or are supposed to have by virtue of 'having lived their lives as women' (Davies and Rosser, 1986, p. 109), for example, tact, compassion, emotional sensitivity. Beauty therapy work is doubly gendered when it deploys these qualities almost exclusively to women in a very female space. However, if beauty therapy is a highly *gendered* work it is not quite *sexualised* work in the sense that Adkins (1995) describes in her study of the tourist industry. Adkins notes that female workers who occupy quite low-grade jobs but who come into contact with the public are required to conform to a very particular code regarding dress and appearance, a code which is not applied to male workers. This code requires women workers to look neat but also reasonably attractive in terms of a conventional heterosexual construction of attractiveness.

Depending upon the type of establishment she is employed within, the beauty therapist is either required to present a clinicised appearance consisting of white overall, subtle make-up and clear or no nail varnish, or she must conform to a more feminised appearance where slightly more colour is allowed in both dress and make-up. All therapists must appear clean and tidy at all times. If beauty therapists depart from the 'clinical' norm for appearance there are dangers in travelling too far in the direction of sexualisation. This is not simply because most of their clients are at present female; in fact several interviewees reported a growing male market, especially for treatments such as waxing body hair. It is precisely because of this growing male market that any sexualisation of the beauty therapist's appearance and persona could be dangerous. Alice, a therapist and salon owner, told me that she had to be very careful when taking on new male clients:

> If we don't know them we say we just do backs. Or if they come on the phone enquiring we say 'just backs'. But if a female client who has been coming regularly recommends they come in then we would extend it to a full body massage. But we wouldn't just say to them on the phone or to some stranger coming in. We have got to be quite careful.
>
> (Alice BT)

In developing the body work side of salon work there is a danger of confusion with the sordid connotations of the massage parlour. This threat must limit the extent to which the therapist can present herself in terms of a sexualised femininity, although clearly it is equally inconceivable that her self-presentation could make no reference to femininity at all.

Is she really a therapist? Emotional labour in the salon

Hochschild defines emotional labour as work which demands that the worker 'induce or suppress feelings in order to sustain the outward countenance that produces the proper state of mind in others' (Hochschild, 1983, p. 7). 'Emotional labour' therefore is about both the emotions of the person who is the 'object' of the labour in question (client/customer/patient) and the emotions of the person who performs that labour. The flight attendants whose work Hochschild studied – like beauty therapists – must induce feelings of comfort, confidence, safety, to make pleasurable an experience which has unpleasant aspects (confinement in a small space, confrontation with the potential risks and dangers of flying;

in the case of beauty therapists, the more trivial but very concrete pains of having the hair ripped from the legs and so on).

Much emotional labour is performed in fulfilment of organisational requirements, especially requirements for orderly and compliant customers/clients/patients. As Treweek (1996) has shown in her study of a nursing home, staff may develop emotional work routines which enable them to 'process' inmates quickly, making the running of the home easier and avoiding disruption, even if they result in some patients' emotional needs being unmet. Yet emotional labour cannot be understood purely in terms of short-term organisational needs. Hochschild is emphatic about the way in which the emotional work of flight attendants is quite explicitly developed and standardised in order to cultivate long-term customer loyalty in a competitive market. Very much the same is true of the work of beauty therapists. Their work is conducted in a commercialised workplace where selling products and retaining a regular long-term clientele are both crucial to the viability of the salon.

Yet there is also a sense in which the emotional work of beauty therapists is, as the therapists themselves often asserted, compared more appropriately to the non-commercial work of nurses. Emotional labour is precisely what we would expect to be required of any group of workers who 'process' other people's bodies. The more intimate the contact with the body, the more the sensitive handling of emotions is likely to be a consideration. It is the failure to do this that is the substance of much critique of doctors. It is the capacity to do this which is such an important part of the professional image of the nurse (Smith, 1992). Beauty therapists are aware that touch is a powerful indicator of intimacy. If the client finds that intimacy difficult to handle, then the therapist must find tactful ways of handling her unease. If that intimacy is welcome, as several interviewees noted, then touch may unleash communication on other levels; the therapist may be required to handle feelings that are not initially and obviously to do with bodies, as, for example, when clients confide about their family or marital problems in the course of a treatment.

More significantly, beauty therapists are aware that some, though by no means all, clients come to the salon with problematic feelings about their bodies – typically insecurity, embarrassment or anxiety about particular features, or consciousness of having failed to live up to the norms of feminine beauty promoted in the public sphere. Interviewees did not regard themselves as party to the promotion of these ideals, or as exploiting these feelings of failure, because they located the pressures to conform to them outside the salon, in the workplace or the media. They presented themselves as allies with the client in helping her to 'make the best of herself' (see Sharma and Black, 1999). According to their own ideology, they conduct therapeutic activities ('treatments') which address the client's subjective feelings quite as much as they address identifiable deficits in appearance, offering the client reassurance and self-confidence.

In Hochschild's analysis, emotional labour is openly recognised as a part of the labour process in a service industry; properly performed it makes the client happy and promotes customer loyalty. Since the emotional work of female flight attendants is explicitly linked to company performance it is not surprising that female flight attendants' bodily performance is closely monitored by the company and that attendants whose appearance and demeanour are deemed deficient will be admonished. The body and person of the flight attendant herself are treated as instruments at the service of the company – with potentially very grave consequences for workers' own health and welfare (Hochschild, 1983; Tyler and Hancock, 2001). This is the ultimate commodification of the person for profit.

The beauty therapist also works at the front line of a commercial venture, and her emotional work is crucial to the success of that venture. However, the expenditure of effort required to manage emotions was not presented as completely problematic. There was certainly recognition that a day on one's feet dealing with other people's needs and feelings could be tiring and stressful:

> At times you can go home . . . you are completely drained because you've been running on empty for half the day, you

know, you're still this happy smiley therapist who's still got to know everything the client asks, yet you've not had anything to eat since nine o'clock and you're absolutely starving.

(Janet BT)

But it was the encounter with feelings – the sense that they had made a client 'feel better' – that was also reported as the source of job satisfaction. It is probably a common case that emotional work brings both stress and satisfaction. Wharton (1993) has criticised Hochschild for overemphasising the psychological and physical cost of the emotional work, and underestimating its satisfactions. She argues that conditions of work are as important as its actual emotional constituents. In particular, the degree of autonomy given to the worker is crucial. Similarly, in both Tyler and Hancock's work and that of Witz *et al.*, little is made of the potential for a sense of professional satisfaction from the engagement in emotional or corporeal labour.

There are certainly a number of factors relating to conditions of work which may account for the beauty therapists' assessment of their emotional work. First, while poorly paid, the work of the beauty therapist does not lend itself to direct or intrusive surveillance, at least in the UK. The therapist typically works in a semi-private cubicle; the client's end-state appearance is visible to the salon owner but s/he is not privy to the transactions that take place in the cubicle. The therapist is presumed to have internalised a degree of professional responsibility such that she can be trusted to work within this necessary privacy. Although this working environment is less evident in countries such as the USA and in the Caribbean, where communal treatment areas are common, the set of professional ethics which includes tending to the emotional well-being of the client means that for beauty therapists, this is seen as a rewarding part of their work, carried out to high professional standards.

Second, the product which the therapist delivers can never be as standardised as the product which the flight attendant delivers. Trade journals may carry articles suggesting formulaic ways of greeting clients, or of suggesting that they buy particular products.

Yet the beauty therapists emphasised that there is always a sense in which she delivers her own style of service; the ways of one therapist may suit one type of client more than another, but provided each therapist builds up a clientele who appreciate her style, the salon will succeed. Indeed, it will succeed better than if it attempts complete standardisation of approach. The individual therapist therefore needs a certain degree of autonomy both to develop her own style and to respond to individual clients' needs within the bounds of the requirements of an orderly salon. This non-standardisation of style and the flexibility to respond to customer needs is one of the characteristics of service work identified by Offe (Offe, 1985; cited in Adkins, 1995, p. 6). The end-product of client satisfaction is the ultimate goal, but the beauty therapist experiences some degree of freedom in delivering that goal.

Third, it seems that few beauty therapists remain in the employment of one salon for long. Many of those who continue as beauty therapists for more than a few years after completing their training will either 'go mobile' (i.e. treat clients in their own homes on a freelance basis), combine 'mobile' work with salon work, or attempt to set up their own salon. Some may combine salon work with mobile work or teaching. To this extent the beauty therapist needs to be something of an individual entrepreneur even while employed by others. This entrepreneurial role is encouraged through training which includes courses on accounting, management and general business skills. She needs to build up a clientele who buy into the particular experience which she and no one else can give them (or so it seems to the client). If she moves between salons or between salon and mobile work, she may expect some of this clientele to follow her. The extent to which the industry is fragmented also allows space for diversity. In salons owned and managed by large conglomerates there is certainly evidence for more uniformity in dress and modes of dealing with clients. However, if the therapist is unhappy with this level of management she is relatively free to move on.

It seems then that the work of the beauty therapist can more usefully be compared to that of health workers or hairdressers rather than the highly regulated world of the commercial service sector as described by Tyler and Hancock or Witz *et al*. All of these factors lead to a situation where the beauty therapist must take a high degree of responsibility for monitoring her own performance as emotional labourer. According to Wharton's analysis, this may account for the fact that beauty therapists see the emotional aspect of their work as a source of satisfaction as well as being physically and emotionally demanding. Although beauty therapists could often cite situations where, like the flight attendants, they were required to engage in deep acting to mask their own feelings, they were fairly free to perform this work in their own way. Those interviewees who were also lecturers stressed the need to encourage responsiveness to the client without resort to formulaic or standardised ('regimental') responses. At all costs the client must not feel that she is on a 'production line'.

Emotional labour is a key element of the work of the beauty therapist, but one which is a source of pride as well as being emotionally and physically draining. However, can we claim that the therapist also performs aesthetic labour? Certainly the body of the beauty therapist is regulated within the work setting. She is taught implicitly and explicitly how to present herself. It is also probably true that women who enter the profession already have an interest in appearance, although increasingly, as some aspects of beauty therapy move closer to complementary therapies, the focus has shifted from looking good to feeling good. However, for all the reasons outlined above, beauty therapy as an industry is not wholly subject to this aestheticisation process. Therapists work in a variety of settings under a wide range of work conditons. Partly as a result of the history which I outlined in chapter 2, the industry is fragmented. Only certain segments of it are controlled by large multinational corporations and, in the small businesses owned and run by beauty therapists themselves, there is less of a formalised system of bodily control. Recruitment may certainly contain an element of selecting the type of worker who 'suits' that business, but again, in the majority of the industry, selection is made through a variety of channels as therapists are judged through work placements, and the high turnover in the industry means that there is not always the degree of choice in the selection process which employers might prefer. Crucially, the industry is also highly feminised not only in terms of its workers, but also its customers. The beauty therapist is not employing aesthetic labour in order to appeal to a predominantly male clientele. Female clients require a very different and finely balanced performance which is not sexualised, is not perceived as 'false' and is in no way about being a 'bimbo with legs up to her armpits'. However, beauty therapy is an industry which is undergoing significant change, including a growing heterosexual male clientele, and this leaves the door open for the recognition and subsequent regulation of the corporeal labour of the therapists to an extent not yet evident in this study.

Emotional labour – an ambivalent resource for therapists

It is an intrinsic characteristic of much emotional labour that it is invisible or unacknowledged and that the consequences of this invisibility are not lost on those who have performed it for many years. This is especially the case where female workers deploy interpersonal skills which are not regarded as resting on any kind of effort or training, but simply as intrinsic to womanhood (and hence do not need to be paid for). The literature on emotional labour that has developed post-Hochschild suggests that the issue of recognition is important. In the flight attendant's work, emotional labour is highly exploitative of the worker's body and feelings, but it is regarded by companies as crucial to customer satisfaction and training is given. More often such recognition and training is not given. Skills in handling emotions are seen as something learned by trial and error on the job, with little explicit training or systematic support. Smith's (1992) study of nursing education showed that while the image of the nurse as caring and sympathetic is salient in recruiting literature and publicity, this recognition is inadequately realised in training programmes, and many student nurses receive little support in developing skills in handling their own and their patients' feelings. In some areas of work the emotional labour is even more invisible, not even articulated in job descriptions or public images of an occupation. This was the case with the hospital administrators studied by Davies and Rosser (1986); the administrators themselves knew that their work involved much tact and imaginative handling of complex situations, especially where they had to deal with distressed patients and their relatives. Yet this side of their work and the skills it involved were invisible in institutional terms since the workers were drawn from a pool of mature women who had generally developed such skills in the course of running a household and raising a family. This is in direct contrast to Witz *et al.*'s study where these skills were made explicit, and indeed constituted part of the training programme for new staff members (Witz *et al.*, 2003). Davies and Rosser note that were this supply of mature recruits to dry up, men or very young women would not be able to do the job in the same way:

> It is not that women do the job and that it gets done in a 'woman's way'; it is not even simply that the qualities of the job and the capabilities of the job holders have become fused. It is rather both that the fusion has occurred and that the fusion itself denigrates and dismissed women's skills.
>
> (Davies and Rosser, 1986, p. 110)

With any other group of workers then, the need to explicitly train for such skills may become more apparent. Beauty therapists are a group of workers striving to reject a public stereotype which, they felt, represented the beauty therapist as some kind of 'bimbo', someone who performed trivial work deploying minor skills, by drawing attention to the emotional labour which was involved in providing 'treatments'. Yet this could be seen as a risky strategy; if emotional work is based on skills which most women automatically acquire through life experience, then this provides a shaky basis for claims to recognition and legitimacy.

It is almost a characteristic of emotional labour that the skills it involves are either unrecognised or simply assumed, especially where female workers are concerned. Where they are recognised there is the danger that emotional drill routines are imposed, such as those which oblige the flight attendant to engage in deep acting, with attendant costs to the labourer. Politically, therefore, the emotional labourer who seeks recognition for his or her labour is between a rock and a hard place.

Servicing the service industries: beauty therapy in the work lives of clients

Beauty salon clients receive treatments which can be classified into types according to the nature of the treatment, the justificatory discourse drawn on by the client, and the area of life which the treatment most obviously supports. I have defined these areas as health treatments; pampering; routine grooming; and corrective. In understanding the work environment of clients, the area of grooming is vital. I have so far discussed the role of emotional labour in beauty therapists' work. I have also outlined debates around the newly aestheticised workplace. Here I will argue that one of the reasons for the growth in the wider beauty industry, the expansion of beauty salons and nail bars, and the growing male market for these products and services, is that the beauty industry services this process. Beauty salons have long been spaces for women to escape to, to be pampered in and to use to maintain an 'appropriate' feminine appearance. They are also spaces where the social rituals of feminine friendship can be cemented. However, one of their increasingly popular functions appears to be the provision of a service to women and men workers in the achievement of a groomed appearance.

Grooming in the workplace

> Perhaps in the working environment, I feel like sometimes I should grow up a bit and growing up seems to mean looking very groomed. . . . And I sort of feel that to be taken seriously I should do something about my hair and put lipstick on and things like that.
>
> (Laura)

Although no men were interviewed in the course of this research, therapists were clear about the types of treatments accessed by male clients. These were referred to predominantly as 'grooming'. In fact the growing male beauty market relies on this term to distinguish its products. In the language of the marketeers, women purchase beauty treatments and men rely on grooming products. Grooming treatments for men in the salon include manicures, facials and waxing of unwanted body hair on the back, chest and shoulders. Grooming for women also includes manicures, eyebrow shaping, facials, eyelash tinting and waxing. These treatments relate to maintaining a general standard of body aesthetics which is not related to vanity or beauty but rather to treatments which might be seen as part of a maintenance routine. An analogy might be the regular servicing of a car which is seen to increase the overall performance of the vehicle and to prevent too rapid a decline in value. Small, regular maintenance functions are carried out which give an overall impression of care having been taken with the body, but without dramatic changes in appearance:

> I think I am happy with myself if I look the best that I can do all of the time. A lot of the time you think, I'll just go out like I am. I think it's best to take the best care of your appearance all the time rather than making yourself look extra special on your Saturday night when you are going out. I think to have an all-round fairly well-kept appearance would be the best thing.
>
> (Nina)

Grooming treatments are often justified in relation to the world of paid employment. If pampering relates to a discourse of stress, 'time for myself' or 'I deserve it' justifications, when discussing the multiple demands placed on the client, then grooming treatments are seen much more as necessities. Where explanation is sought it is received in terms of an 'acceptable' standard of appearance, with the 'acceptable' standard being related to expectations within the workplace. Time saving may also be drawn upon. If manicures and so on are seen as a necessary routine, then having an expert perform this function may save time. The effects last longer and take less time to achieve. Similarly, eyebrow shaping or eyelash tinting may reduce the need for make-up, thus saving valuable minutes in the morning prior to work.

> I'd maybe have a facial and always have my eyelashes dyed, but that was to do with work and looking smart, and it actually saves a bit of time if you have your eyelashes dyed.
>
> (Madeleine)

Grooming treatments are a staple of the evening, lunch-time and weekend trade in salons as both male and female workers receive treatments which fit in with their employment routine, and their own bodily maintenance programmes:

> This is why we've got a bit of a gap and then all of a sudden they're haring in for a quick half leg [wax] and an eyebrow trim and then dash back to work.
>
> (Yvette BT)

Aestheticisation at work

If grooming for clients is related to the world of work, then this grooming process is highly gendered. Much has been made of a supposed feminisation of the workplace, and the workforce (Massey, 1984; Jenson *et al.*, 1988). Here it is argued that, for example, in Western Europe since the 1980s there has been an increasing rate of workplace participation for women, and a decreasing rate for men. Accompanying these changes have also been a restructuring in the types of employment available with an increase in service sector employment and a decrease in the traditional industries and heavy manufacturing. More recent arguments have begun to question some of the assumptions of these feminisation arguments. A clear example has been a closer examination of what it is about service sector jobs which actually relates to feminising. Why are caring and servicing necessarily regarded as female skills within a labour market when in fact the divisions between gendered skills is shifting and complex (Adkins, 2001)?

In contrast, Adkins argues that it is more useful to think through these processes in terms of an 'aestheticisation'. The primacy of appearance, image and style in certain workplaces is, she argues, less related to the feminisation of skills and more to the processes whereby skills are recognised and rewarded in the workplace. This process remains highly gendered and has not benefited women as much as some of the feminisation arguments might suggest.

The notion of 'performance' in the work environment has, according to Adkins and Lury (2000), been used in three key ways. First, in relation to the ways in which work is increasingly individualised and requires the reflexivity of self-creation in order to succeed. Here, for example, Beck (1992) argues that class or gender are now less important in determining labour market status than this individualised process. Second, performativity refers to the dramaturgical structure of service sector work. Hochschild's discussion of emotional labour may be usefully understood in this tradition. Finally, the term refers to the increasing reference to style, appearance and self-presentation in the contemporary organisation (Adkins and Lury, 2000, p. 164). It is in this latter sense that Adkins and Lury situate their work.

They begin with Lash and Urry's (1994) claim that aesthetic and emotional aspects of labour are becoming increasingly important in relation to a previous focus on technical aspects of production. This may be read as mirroring the move from a manufacturing to a service- or consumption-based economy. This shift is accompanied by a process of individualisation where the reflexive subject becomes a product of this process of 'de-traditionalization' (Lash and Urry, 1994, pp. 4–5, cited in Adkins and Lury, 2000, p. 152). Workplace techniques which contribute to this shift include intensification of management of the corporeal aspects of employees and increasing interventions in the emotional lives of workers.

What Adkins and Lury achieve is to show how these processes do not simply reward the performative skills learned and displayed by workers sensitive to these requirements and also increasingly subject to their management. Instead, they argue that valued workplace identities are not universally available. The self-directed, stress-managed, well-groomed and ambitious worker who embodies the ethos of the corporation is a highly gendered project. In short, when men perform this labour they are rewarded for their efforts. Young men in particular are becoming increasingly aware of the rewards to be derived from achieving this workplace identity. In contrast, when women invest significant amounts of time, effort and economic outlay in achieving a similar performance their labour is seen less as a skill to be rewarded, and more as an immanent feminine characteristic. When women achieve what is demanded of them through the highly regulated work environment they are seen to be simply performing feminised and naturalised female characteristics. When they do not manage their corporeal being correctly they are punished. For example, Madeleine described a series of encounters with her male boss which amounted to a campaign of bullying. The ridicule which he subjected her to centred around her appearance:

> I hadn't realised I had got so scrappy. It was embarrassing. They [employer] literally compared me with this other woman who is immaculate and groomed and they just said, 'Well look at her'. And I just stood there in reception and I felt really humiliated. I just wanted the ground to swallow me up. Did I look that scruffy? I couldn't have looked that bad but it really hurt.

Here we are faced with the gulf in significance between the female worker dyeing her eyelashes and the male executive's manicure. However, it is also the case that male bodies are becoming commodified in an unprecedented form. While women's bodies have been subject to commodification and objectification, men's bodies too are increasingly being brought into the system of exchange. It is this commodification element which is crucial to validating any arguments around aestheticisation. It is also vital in understanding how men are rewarded for body work while women are not. Adkins and Lury echo Witz *et al.*'s claim concerning the spread of workplace performances based on corporeality, arguing that management of the self has become a commodity which can be exchanged for pay in the market place.

However, both remuneration and sanction are clearly relative to position in the workforce and gender identity. For male workers the efforts of bodily investment are recognised; for women the performance is not recognised as such unless it is somehow transgressive.

Beauty therapy – grooming the service worker

Beauty therapy is part of a growing beauty industry. It offers a range of treatments which fulfil different roles in clients' lives. In this regard, beauty therapy may be seen as a service industry servicing the service industry in that it offers treatments which are required to either avoid sanction or gain reward in the workplace. Other service industries are growing up around these requirements. For example, image consultancy is an integral part of the type of employment described by Witz *et al.* as 'interactive service work' (Witz *et al.*, 2003, p. 35). Wellington and Bryson (2001) outline three areas in which image consultancies have been brought in to offer services in the workplace. First, employees in the clothing retail sector are provided with the 'confidence and expertise' to advise potential customers about their clothing requirements (p. 939). Second, consultations are used to restructure the bodies of professionals. This might be thought of as a 'make-over' in the popular sense. Employees not only benefit from this 'confidence boost' but also learn to project a more professional and corporatised image through dress and appearance. Finally, workshops are provided for staff who come into direct contact with clients, and here the consultants provide an extension of training in customer service. Wellington and Bryson point out that the overwhelming majority of corporate and private clients of these consultancies are women. Clearly, the fact that this is a growing industry indicates the demand for such services in an 'aestheticised' economy. As workers themselves are acutely aware of any skill which will give them an advantage in a competitive market, they are turning

increasingly to the informal image consultant – the beauty therapist. Here the traditional 'pampering' service of the beauty therapist
is being extended to include new types of treatments, to include
women who would not previously have visited a salon, and also
to include men who are becoming aware of the advantages of an
investment in body capital in the workplace.

To what extent could the beauty salon clients in this study be
described as part of an aestheticised economy? They certainly
experienced rules about suitable dress and appearance in the workplace. However, there did appear to be some flexibility, with
expectations varying according to the level of face-to-face contact
with the public, or with more formal dress being required when
representing the company in meetings with clients. For those
employed in non-manufacturing sectors, this contact with the
public, or the level of responsibility for representing their
employer, was the key factor in deciding the regulation of their
dress and demeanour. However, the somaticised performance of a
company ethos was not fully evident in the ways that interviewees
described their workplace appearance. This could be of course that
the clients included in this study, and the types of salons selected,
did not encompass the workers in the specific sector of the service
industries where these processes are most evident. Witz *et al.* leave
unspecific their definition of what constitutes the 'cutting edge
sector' they discuss, but both they and Tyler and Hancock claim
that these practices are supposedly spreading more widely.

What was very clear from speaking to beauty salon clients was
the amount of regulation which centred on gender, and to some
extent class performance in the workplace. To return to the
example of Madeleine above who experienced harassment in her
place of work. The comments on her appearance centred around
a class-based aesthetic. She came from a middle-class background,
and although currently lacking in economic capital, she did possess
high levels of cultural capital in terms of her accent, interest in the
arts and travel. However, as a product of this specific class location,
her dress centred around being 'smart' without exhibiting an
investment in appearance, either in terms of time or economic

outlay. Thus her clothes were purchased from secondhand shops and she wore no make-up. Her boss at the time of interview was a working–class man employed in an engineering company where she was a receptionist. The critique of her dress code then was as much a clash over class background and the relative display of 'taste' as it was about the aestheticised workplace. Being seen as feminine and smart were not enough to avoid sanction. What was required in this context was the explicit display of a class-based femininity which reflected the clientele, managers and employees of the company. This is thus an example of employment in what could be described in terms of a traditional manufacturing sector which is deliberately excluded from the analysis of the new service sector. However, Madeleine's role as receptionist in the company placed her in a visible position in greeting clients. Among the interviewees it was this visible role which predisposed employer regulation of appearance.

While Adkins and Lury are excellent in showing how reflexivity and the self-created worker is a highly gendered and particularly heterosexualised identity, they are less clear in making explicit the role of class in claiming such an identity. This is partly because they draw upon work which is keen to emphasise the worker in contemporary Western capitalism as engaged in a project of reflexively creating the self (Lash and Urry, 1994). This atomised worker is less likely to be embedded in traditional social relations such as class, and more likely to experience the market directly from within shifting allegiances. While Adkins and Lury dismiss key elements of the feminisation thesis as leaving unchallenged presumptions around what are feminine and masculine roles and skills, there is actually some strength to such arguments when class is added to the analysis. Thus, for example, Lovell (2000) argues that:

> There is some evidence that femininity as cultural capital is beginning to have broader currency in unexpected ways. Demand for stereotypically feminine skills is generally increasing on the labour market.
>
> (Lovell, 2000, p. 25)

As the labour market shifts to a dominance of employment in the service sector:

> Working-class femininity may begin to have a competitive market advantage compared with the attributes of traditional working-class masculinity.
>
> (ibid.)

By focusing on working-class identities we can see that traditionally masculine skills which were valued in the manufacturing sector are becoming increasingly redundant. This has been allied to an expanding service or administrative sector which requires the skills that are more likely to be possessed by working-class women than by working-class men. A focus on the service sector then is also a study in the relative value of classed identities.

Although the evidence from this study is not strong enough to be conclusive, I would speculate that as service employment expands, women from a variety of backgrounds are being drawn into this type of employment. This has occurred to a greater extent among working-class women than among working-class men. In this sense, Lovell is correct to claim femininity as an increasingly valuable cultural capital, in this limited sense. However, the regulation of the body demanded in this sector has previously relied on the aesthetic taste schema of the petit bourgeoisie (Bourdieu, 1984). With the expansion of the service industries, and particularly those which require interaction between employee and customer, more women are finding it necessary to access the grooming services provided by the beauty industry. They are also more likely to engage in other pursuits related to health and well-being which have become part of the leisure time of employees. While petit-bourgeois women previously might have made use of the services of a beauty therapist, the members of a newly expanding strata of the middle class, sometimes labelled the 'service class' (Butler, 1995), are also turning to beauty therapy. I would speculate that previously working-class women are being drawn into this type of employment, and they in turn make use of the services of the beauty salon. In this somaticised service sector, men too are experiencing the increased management of their bodies, but they are disproportionately reaping the rewards of their investment.

In this way beauty therapy may be seen to feed into a newly aestheticised and performative work environment. Where value is placed on appearance and self-regulation, it is necessary for both the woman worker and the woman therapist to invest in these commodities. It is also increasingly necessary for men. The beauty salon has experienced a boom, along with body-based leisure activities, in its role of servicing the service industries.

Chapter 5

Look good, feel better

Promoting health in the beauty salon

The title 'look good, feel better' refers to the publicity for a project which runs in a hospital in one of the research sites. Patients in a cancer ward are given beauty treatments and offered advice on make-up and wigs, as cancer treatment can result in hair loss. The 'look good, feel better' programme aims to provide a 'confidence boost' to the patient through attention to the body. Although these treatments take place in a medicalised setting they are emphatically not about treatment in a bio-medical sense, but rather contribute to a general sense of wellness.

In the salon too, health treatments form part of the range of services on offer. Clients access the salon in order to alleviate the symptoms of chronic conditions such as Multiple Sclerosis (MS) and also to contribute to a more holistic sense of well-being. I will first address these differences in understanding how clients use the salon for health treatments and place these claims within the framework of the concept of the 'healthy lifestyle'. Beauty therapists compare themselves to health workers, most often to nurses. I investigate the claims of the beauty therapist in relation to her professional status and how she contributes to the health of her clients. Beauty therapists describe their work as focusing both upon the body and feelings. They claim to fulfil a counselling role with their clients which aids emotional health and in turn improves physical health. The work of the beauty therapist may be understood through her relationships with the medical profession, and with other complementary therapies. It seems that although there is increasing co-operation between the therapist and the bio-medical establishment, beauty therapy may more usefully be understood as offering a set of complementary therapies and as contributing to the leisure and consumption practices which constitute the 'healthy lifestyle'.

What is health?

As has been pointed out in several contexts, sociologists and anthropologists have long been concerned with illness, and only more recently concerned with health (Saltonstall, 1993; Nettleton, 1995). This is partly because some definitions of health have centred upon notions of absence of illness and disease. Such negative definitions take the lead from a medical perspective. More recently, the World Health Organisation (WHO) has offered a (rather idealistic) positive definition of what constitutes health as 'a state of complete physical, mental and social well-being' (Nettleton, 1995, p. 41). In practice, it is not easy to separate out bio-medical, holistic and lay perceptions of health. Lay definitions contain elements of bio-medicine, which is understandable given that the lay population derive their understandings of health within a society where bio-medicine dominates. The medical profession itself also combines both bio-medical and more holistic approaches to the health of their patients.

Lay understandings are notoriously complex, sometimes contradictory, and difficult to define. Early studies distinguished between a negative concept (the absence of illness or disease) and a positive view (health which comes from within). Health was seen to be made up of three different elements: the absence of disease, a 'reserve' of health determined by individual temperament and constitution, and a positive state of well-being (cited in Blaxter, 1990, p. 14). Other studies have generally found similar distinctions among lay perception, although the predominance of any particular view is dependent upon social position.

In Blaxter's survey of the health and lifestyles of the UK population several broad categories applicable to oneself or to others emerged from the data (Blaxter, 1990). First, 'negative' answers found the concept of health difficult to define, and the respondents often could not think of anyone known to them who was healthy. An additional dimension to this view was that because health is so much the norm, so much a part of taken-for-granted everyday life, then being asked to define it created difficulties. Second, health was defined in negative terms as the absence of illness or disease. Blaxter argues, in contradiction to other studies, that this concept was not differentially distributed according to economic status. Its use was, however, closely associated with the health status of the respondent. Almost paradoxically, older respondents and those suffering from chronic conditions were less likely to define health in terms of lack of illness. Health was also defined as the capacity to be well even when disease was present. Thus, for example, those who were suffering from a condition but who were not experiencing symptoms could be seen as healthy. Those who were coping well with a chronic condition might also be seen to be healthy in lay terms. Next, health was seen as a reserve, or the capacity to recover well from illness. Health was also defined in terms of a 'healthy lifestyle'. Young people especially were likely to define a healthy person as 'someone who doesn't smoke or drink'. Respondents drawing on this view often mentioned health in terms of personal responsibility and associated moral responsibility with the avoidance of illness. Health was also seen in terms of physical fitness. Again, this concept was favoured by the young and was less likely to be mentioned by men and women over age 60. Blaxter points out that this association of health with physical strength is one of the reasons why the sex of a person most likely to be thought of as healthy was seen as male by both men and women (Blaxter, 1990, p. 24). Health as energy or vitality combines physical strength or wellness with psychological well-being. Here the focus is on a positive mental attitude and the sense of being 'full of life' (p. 25). One of the notable differences between men and women was that women were much more likely to define health in terms of social relationships. Men who included social factors did so in relation to their own moods and how their health impacted upon these moods and their relationship with others. In contrast, women of all ages were more likely to locate definitions of their own health in terms of their social relations with others. Feelings of well-being impacted positively on their capacity to care for and relate to others. Health as a function combines both health as energy and health as social relationships in that when both of these factors are present the person is able to perform social functions and to cope with their various roles in everyday life. Finally, health was seen as psychosocial well-being. Although this category is closely related to earlier descriptions of energy, or social relationships, it is reserved for the purely psychological state independent of physical factors. Psychosocial factors were often embedded in a holistic view. Feeling happy and relaxed were phrases important to both men and women.

This outline of the differing aspects of health from one study in the UK shows how complex the definition and measurement of health actually is. As Calnan has pointed out, definitions of health in the abstract may bear little resemblance to the definitions used to guide everyday practice. For this reason he argues that more functional concepts of health predominate on a day-to-day level (Calnan, 1994, p. 75).

What is important to note here, however, is that illness and health may be understood separately in terms of related behaviour. Thus, for example, engaging in a 'healthy lifestyle' will not necessarily prevent the onset of disease:

> Social action relating to health and social action relating to disease are not necessarily the same thing in that they may be logically separate and based on distinct forms of reasoning. Ideas about the causation of disease are therefore not the same as ideas about the maintenance of health, as might previously have been supposed.
>
> (Nettleton, 1995, p. 45)

This distinction is important to remember when understanding the health-related activities of beauty salon clients, and in how therapists understand their own contribution to health. As I will discuss below, clients may visit the salon for alleviation of the symptoms of disease. However, their visits are much more likely to be described in terms of contributing to a general sense of health. Correspondingly, beauty therapists may emphasise their relationship with the medical profession, but it is more likely to be in relation to their view of themselves as holistic therapists, rather than in any bio-medical sense.

These definitions of health emphasise differing aspects of human experience. They have in common an increasing broadness and a move away from medicalised notions towards what might be termed more 'holistic' conceptions of what it means to be healthy. The increasing range of definitions also means that more and more areas of life may be defined in relation to the health of the individual. Thus, for example, we are now able to speak of healthy or unhealthy *lifestyles*. The WHO defines lifestyle as:

> A general way of living based on the interplay between living conditions in the widest sense and individual patterns of behaviour as determined by socio-cultural factors and personal characteristics.
>
> (Health Education Unit, WHO, 1993, p. 229)

This conception of lifestyle includes both the widest social context and the individual's own actions, so incorporating virtually every area of life into our attempts to understand and define 'health'. To some extent this indicates that the WHO has taken on the language of market research companies as well as the social sciences in referring to a coherent identity which we might recognise as a lifestyle. Although the definition carefully includes wider social context, the concept of lifestyle in other uses focuses on an individualised set of actions for which the person is increasingly responsible. This WHO definition of lifestyle differs from the term as used in social science in that it is less allied to a particular understanding of contemporary society. I will return to the issue of lifestyle below, but it should be noted that the role of the beauty salon becomes vital in understanding client experiences of health and well-being, as the salon and the health-promoting activities carried out there are firmly intertwined with the wider life situation of the client.

Who is healthy?

Following the WHO emphasis on the importance of social factors in defining and measuring health, we can investigate the relative social positions of those who are more or less healthy. In examining class differences, for example, Savage *et al.* (1992) describe distinctions between segments of the middle classes which relate to occupation and income. Following Bourdieu (Bourdieu, 1984, 1990), they outline the relative amounts of economic and cultural capital possessed by these classes, and argue that by focusing on class differences we can understand consumption patterns and distinctive lifestyles. They describe three salient types of middle-class lifestyle: the ascetic, the postmodern and the undistinctive. Although these may be influenced by gender and age, their salient features hold. The undistinctive lifestyle is associated with what may be termed 'organisation man', and is adopted particularly by managers and government bureaucrats. These workers are relatively detached from the market place and have been able to rely on secure employment. Their interests lie in conventional sports such as fishing, sailing and golf, and in pursuing leisure time enjoying the countryside (Savage *et al.*, 1992, p. 116). In contrast, the ascetic lifestyle is adopted by those working in the public welfare sector who possess relatively high cultural capital and low economic capital. The characteristics of this way of life include engagement with a 'healthy' lifestyle and involvement in various body projects. The development of an identity based around the body allows storage of cultural assets in bodily form, compensating for a lack of economic assets, or access to the stability and security of employment experienced by managers and bureaucrats. The investment in cultural capital also extends to enjoyment of 'foreign' food and travel. Finally, the postmodern lifestyle contains elements of the culture of excess and indulgence associated with high income and also aspects of the ascetic lifestyle as it relates to health and body maintenance. These types of individuals are to be found in professions such as law, financial services, personnel, economic advice, marketing, advertising and financial advice (ibid., p. 115). These professionals possess the economic capital to allow conspicuous consumption, and the cultural capital to engage in 'appreciation' of traditionally elite cultural forms. This lifestyle has adopted ascetic approaches to health but has interpreted these in a commodified form.

It is perhaps the ascetic lifestyle which comes closest to an ideal in terms of promoting and maintaining health. Savage *et al.* are not directly concerned with questions of health, but their typology may be used to understand how experiences of health and well-being are related to lifestyles, which within their theoretical framework are in turn the product of relative social positioning. Although their ascetic lifestyle is useful in understanding the commodification of bodies and practices in the pursuit of health, the description 'ascetic' might be slightly misleading. What is missing is a recognition that at least some of the body practices engaged in are intensely pleasurable and are pursued for this reason in addition to any advancement of cultural assets. Massage is a good example of a practice that can be claimed as a leisure form which contributes to bodily capital, at the same time as offering a degree of sensuality and pleasure to the recipient.

In her national survey of the health-related activities and attitudes of British citizens in the late 1980s, Blaxter does link together lifestyles with health-related behaviour. She includes four key measures of behaviour which are associated with a 'good' or healthy lifestyle (Blaxter, 1990). I have outlined above the lay perceptions of health which emerged from this study. The respondents in the survey most likely not to smoke, drink to excess, eat a healthy diet and to take regular exercise were women aged 18 to 39. However, what is interesting in terms of Savage *et al.*'s claims is that such a lifestyle was also associated with higher income, higher educational qualifications and professional or technical occupations. Although Blaxter's schema is not directly comparable to Savage *et al.*'s, there does seem to be some overlap in the groups described as engaging in ascetic (Savage *et al.*) or good (Blaxter) lifestyles in relation to health. It is also worth noting that their research was conducted over a similar time-scale, suggesting further that they were uncovering the formation of particular cultural practices into newly emerging lifestyles closely associated with transformations in class structure in the UK.

Blaxter notes a positive association between a healthy lifestyle and women. Savage *et al.* are less clear, although they do point to an association of middle-class women with yoga, keep-fit, riding and participation in health clubs, contrasting this to the competitive and team sports enjoyed by men. Although Savage *et al.*'s typology may go some way towards explaining the preferences of salon clients according to their class position, they are less successful in taking gender into account.

More recent work, although based on longitudinal data from 1984 and 1992, is that undertaken by Tomlinson (2003). His analysis of the UK *Health and Lifestyles Survey* supports his view that health-related behaviour is associated with social class. This remains true over the time period covered by the data, and a weakening association between the two is not in evidence. He segments his data into four quadrants based on behaviour such as alcohol consumption, smoking and participation in sport. These are labelled 'unhealthy', 'active', 'healthy' and 'sober', and show how 'there exists in these data a set of distinct health-related lifestyles' (Tomlinson, 2003, p. 102). Lifestyles are related to social hierarchy, although age and gender also have an impact. Healthier behaviours are associated with higher social class, women and older age groups. Women tend to be more healthy than men across all classes, even though, between women, a class divide is evident.

If we take the widest definitions of health, it is clear that activities such as keep-fit, attention to diet and interest in complementary therapies are associated with particular lifestyles which are becoming more widespread in contemporary British society and in other industrialised countries. As Crawford incisively comments:

> The health enthusiasts, those proclaiming by example and advocacy a healthy life style, appear to be overwhelmingly middle class. Whilst working class struggles to shorten the work week, abolish child labour, and change working conditions have historically in part focused on health, and although occupational health and safety has also generated a

new interest in recent years, the current preoccupation with personal health displays a distinctive – although not exclusive – middle class stamp.

(Crawford, 1980, p. 365)

It is to the explanations of how we might make sense of this widening perception of health that I now turn.

Medicalisation, governmentality and the 'healthy lifestyle'

The pieces of research outlined above may be placed in a wider theoretical context which enables us to understand the medical profession, the idea of health and the concept of a lifestyle. These approaches offer conflicting interpretations of health. The medicalisation critique emerged from Marxist and liberal humanist traditions in the 1960s and 1970s (Lupton, 1997). This critique centres on two paradoxical characteristics of modern medicine. First, medical interventions could be seen to be ineffective and in some cases even harmful to health. Illich, for example, contends that medicine is iatrogenic in that it leads to harmful side effects which worsen health. In addition, the fostering of dependence on the medical profession removes autonomy from the lay population and decreases the capacity for self-care (Illich, 1975). Second, despite these negative consequences the medical profession has expanded its sphere of influence and increased its power. Freidson outlines both the autonomy and dominance of the medical profession which contribute to medicalisation (Freidson, 1970). Increasingly, social problems come to be seen through the prism of medicine and defined in bio-medical rather than social or political terms. In this sense then the medical profession takes on the role of social regulation. This role may be seen to correspond to the increasing tendency to offer scientific explanations more generally as the power of tradition and organised religion (particularly Christianity) has declined. In these senses contemporary society may be described as increasingly medicalised.

The consequence of the increasing power vested in medical professionals is a corresponding decrease in the power and autonomy of lay people. For example, ageing and diet are increasingly subject to scientific discourses and removed from the realm of everyday knowledge. Illness caused by poverty and other social inequality also becomes medicalised and depoliticised. Second, the expertise and knowledge claimed by the medical profession serve to exclude those who are not experts – again fostering dependency and removing the ability to act independently. Critics of this process have generally proposed a 'demedicalisation' of society. This may entail increased state regulation of the practices of the medical professions. Empowerment of lay people and patients is also advocated either through engagement in preventive health practices or through challenging the status and decisions of professionals.

This medicalisation critique may be seen to present a rather simplistic and monolithic view of the 'medical profession' which does not fit with the fragmented and specialised sphere of health care. For example, the British population is increasingly turning to alternative or complementary medicine (Budd and Sharma, 1994). Where would the ancillary industries of health education, gyms and even beauty therapy fit into a simplified conception of health professionals? The medicalisation approach has touched upon transformations in contemporary health care systems, but has in fact got the arguments the wrong way round. Rather than seeing bio-medicine as the driving force for change, we can see that, as the medical profession has expanded into more areas of life, it in turn has been drawn into wider transformative processes and been influenced by them. It is also the case that modern medicine is not simply iatrogenic and disempowering. Health benefits for individuals and for populations as a whole have resulted from developments in bio-medicine. It seems disingenuous to deny these benefits in presenting an idealised critique. As some Foucauldian arguments have shown, there is also a danger with advocating 'empowerment' of patients and lay people (Lupton, 1997). By transferring responsibility for health away from professional bodies, the concept can become further individualised. It can also evolve into a different type of control rather than liberation:

Thus the move towards 'demedicalisation' may be interpreted paradoxically as a growing penetration of the clinical gaze into the everyday lives of citizens, including their emotional states, the nature of their interpersonal relationships, their management of 'stress' and their 'lifestyle' choices.

(Lupton, 1997, p. 107)

To understand this critique we must draw upon different notions of power, and of the self. Following Foucault, arguments around governmentality of the body point out that it is not that the medical profession somehow distorts potentially healthy bodies and practices through its own domination, but rather that medical knowledge and its practitioners are constituitive of both bodies and subjectivities (Foucault, 1990, 1991). Power here is not seen as a zero sum game where the gains of the medical profession represent a corresponding disempowering of the lay population. Instead, for Foucault, power is seen as an infinite characteristic of all aspects of social life. It cannot be seen as repressing some natural essence of the body or health, as to presume such a 'natural' state is to ignore the fact that no pre-social body or state of being can be known or attained. Rather we should see the social relations in which we are embedded and the operation of power as creating and defining the very entities which we think of as 'the body' or 'health'. The role of the medical profession here is of course key, and Foucault outlines the increasing dominance of the profession from the seventeenth century (Foucault, 1991). He also outlines the development of discourses by and through the medical profession which serve to create the field within which they operate. In this approach the medical profession is constituted by a loosely linked set of discourses, practices and sites:

The central strategies of disciplinary power are observation, examination, measurement and the comparison of individuals against an established norm, bringing them into a field of visibility. It is exercised not primarily through direct coercion or violence (although it must be emphasised that these strategies are still used from time to time), but rather through persuading its subjects that certain ways of behaving and thinking are appropriate for them.

(Lupton, 1997, p. 99)

The governance of the body pervades all aspects of social life and is not simply a characteristic of the medical sphere. For this reason it is not necessarily positive that Western populations are turning increasingly to complementary therapies, as these in themselves may also perpetuate the surveillance of the body, and are a symptom of micro power relations. These forms of discourse pervade all relations and practices in the form of surveillance and the operations of power. In contrast to the medicalisation thesis, it is not possible to remove power from members of the medical profession and transfer it to patients or lay people. Power is not inherent to particular groups, and cannot be possessed as such. Rather all are caught in a disciplinary, and medicalised, set of discourses which regulate thought, behaviour and appearance. There is some debate as to what extent such a theory allows for resistance and change. It is possible to read from Foucault's approach a very docile and disciplined body. Foucault did emphasise the contestable nature of power and its productive potential, claiming that where there is power there is also the possibility of resistance. However, he was less clear on how this resistance might occur and what strategies might be involved. He is also notoriously ambiguous on questions of gender and 'race' (Ramazanoglu, 1993). In discussions of 'the body' or 'health' it is clearly inadequate to fail to address the differences in what might constitute 'normality' in relation to these identities. Finally, while deeply concerned with bodily practices it is possible to lose site of the lived fleshy body in arguments about discourses and practices.

Although both of these approaches have been popular within the sociology of medicine in understanding the operation of the medical profession and lay perceptions of health, I am pursuing a different explanatory framework in making sense of health treatments in the beauty salon, and here it is necessary to return to the concept of the 'healthy lifestyle'. Tomlinson (2003) outlines three major positions with regard to food consumption. In doing so he neatly summarises differing approaches to understanding consumption practices in relation to lifestyle. It is his first and third positions that are most useful for my discussion. His first position is:

> The Bourdieu (1984) thesis which suggests that different classes exhibit different lifestyles that in some sense reflect their class position in society due to differing levels of social, economic and cultural capital.
>
> (Tomlinson, 2003, p. 97)

His third position:

> Is the 'post-Fordist' school, which suggests that as the era of mass consumption disappears lifestyles become more and more diverse. This idea, fuelled by reflexive sociology and notions of culture, suggests that traditional class-related consumption patterns should be disappearing as people no longer wish to be associated with a mass or class in the old sense.
>
> (ibid., p. 98)

Tomlinson lists Beck (1992) and Lash and Urry (1994) as exponents of this latter view. As I outlined above, Tomlinson then goes on to show how health behaviour in UK society may be shown to correspond to social class position. He is dismissive of the claims by writers of the 'post-Fordist' type who emphasise the self-reflexivity inherent in viewing lifestyle as a project of actively creating the self through consumption choices. The individualisation inherent in this perception of society creates a loosely associated set of individuals who are able to form alliances across old antagonisms or disparities (Beck, 1992). For Tomlinson, this position is not supported by empirical evidence, at least in relation to food consumption and health practices. In this sense the 'healthy lifestyle' is the product of dispositions which guide behaviour, rather than the more fluid self-reflexivity to be found in newer forms of identification. This use of healthy lifestyle is in keeping with earlier arguments I have made concerning the production of femininity in the salon. I am cautious about ascribing disposition in the Bourdieu sense to class alone, and in fact Tomlinson himself shows how women across classes are more likely to be health conscious than men, and older people undertake more healthy behaviour than those younger than themselves. However, if we combine a sense of classed disposition with my earlier arguments about appropriateness which are more specifically related to gender, we begin to see that health treatments in the salon are a product of a feminised identity within a particular 'lifestyle' which in turn depends on social position. It is within this context that I will now explore the health-related treatments provided in the salon.

Health treatments in the beauty salon

Practices in the salon which are described as 'health treatments' may be further divided into those which are accessed in order to alleviate the symptoms of medically recognised illnesses, and those which the clients describe as contributing to a more general and holistic sense of well-being. It should be noted that all clients 'felt better' after their treatment in the salon, either because they had claimed time for themselves through pampering, had corrected some aspect of their appearance which caused them concern, or had invested in a grooming treatment which would contribute to their appearance in the workplace. I am not referring here to the positive effects of these treatments, but to the specific claims concerning the improvement of physical or emotional health made by clients who undertook what they described as health treatments.

Medical conditions alleviated are often those which can be treated by a medical professional but are not a priority for the National Health Service (NHS). Sometimes it is recognised by General Practitioners (GPs) that treatment by a beauty therapist is a good alternative. Two of the therapists interviewed had worked for the 'look good, feel better' project where cancer patients in hospitals were given massages, and also advice on make-up and using wigs in cases where treatment had led to hair loss. Two therapists had worked for mental health charities giving treatments to people with mental illness. Two clients, Judith and Sandra, described visits to beauty salons for the alleviation of symptoms for serious medical conditions. Judith's GP recommended massage for treatment of Repetitive Strain Injury (RSI). She also received reflexology. In this case massage and other complementary therapies were also available at the GP practice:

> She [doctor] seems to be one of these that believe in alternative remedies, or even trying alternatives to see. But I think most of the group practices have alternative medicine groups within their practices. Even from our own doctors, if they feel that acupuncture or reflexology would be of benefit and they have it in their practice, you can have half an hour trying it.
>
> (Judith)

Sandra visited the salon for massages and claimed that they greatly relieved the symptoms of her Multiple Sclerosis (MS). However, her GP was more sceptical, and she had found the medical profession in general unhelpful:

> I've worked in the health service, directly with the medical profession, and was quite appalled by their attitude to me when I did start to be ill. And having been such an active person, the fact that I wasn't able to exercise, and treated me a bit like a hypochondriac or perhaps having some sort of nervous breakdown or that sort of thing. It was very upsetting. In the end I sort of gave the medical profession the elbow and decided to try and do things which I felt would help me.

It was for this reason that Sandra had begun to receive treatments from beauty therapists and other complementary therapists, which she found extremely beneficial:

> I am sort of aware which part or which muscles are bothering me and I know when she [therapist] starts working on them, how she releases them. When she starts off it can be quite

painful and by the time she has finished they just feel a lot less painful and easier for me. When you have lived with it [MS] for a long time you tend to get on with it but it's not until you have had a massage and all those bits have been released that you realise just how bad they were before.

In the second sense of health, other clients received massage, aromatherapy and reflexology. They describe these treatments in less formal, medical terms and more in terms of well-being. A discourse of holism is drawn on to describe the physical and psychological benefits obtained:

No, no pain. It's nurturing things for me.

(Suki)

The importance of this holistic view of health often emerged from changing life circumstances, perhaps a means of coping with the ageing process, or as a method of making sense of a transitional period. For example, the experience of pregnancy had emphasised Suki's concern for her own physical and emotional health:

I hear stories from my friends who have babies and they lived in a world of just sleep and being like a zombie and I thought I would really like to get as much time in now relaxing and getting ready for the baby mentally as much as anything else.

An earlier set of treatments had centred around her marriage and she was now preparing for the important event of giving birth in a similar way:

I don't often grow my nails but then when I do, again that's a special thing, and for my wedding and again now when I'm pregnant, I am relaxing.

The nail growth is a symbol of disengagement from the ordinary routines of work and life and a commitment to focusing on other priorities:

> Massage feels very calming. It feels like taking time out from my busy life to do those things for myself. It feels very nurturing.
>
> (Suki)

This turn to health-related treatments was a product of moving through the lifecourse and specific trigger events:

> In my teenage years I was very self-conscious and aware of appearance, and tried lots of creams and make-ups and my body came second really. But as I have got older my views on appearance have changed. I think because I am more self-assured now. As an adult I have got much more to base my confidence on rather than just appearance so the salon has formed more a part of the health thing.
>
> (Suki)

For Joanne, treatments in the salon were allied to a change in her exercise and eating habits as well as a reduction in her alcohol consumption. These changes had been set in motion as a response to her changing work situation which she defined as a process of becoming more 'grown-up':

> A full body massage is about thirty to forty pounds so it's quite a decadent thing. Since I've been earning a bit more money, but probably linked to that is more stress, and I've noticed that I'm becoming much more aware of my physical well-being and my emotional well-being and that is what I really like about massage because it really does concentrate on both.

Joanne had recently received a promotion at work and had also just passed her 28th birthday. She described how because of these two events she felt that 'I need to start looking after myself a bit more now'. As a result, massages, control of diet, restriction of alcohol intake and an exercise programme were all introduced into her life routine. Again, earlier salon use had centred on special occasions such as weddings, but with career progression the emphasis in treatments changed. It is interesting to note that at her request our interview was conducted in a local health food restaurant where I drank coffee and she sipped freshly squeezed orange juice. Massages in the salon were seen to contribute to health in that 'it detoxifies you, and is good for your circulation and your skin tone'. However, the major health benefit was seen to come from the relaxation which it gave rise to. In this sense health was judged both in physical and psychological terms. The beauty salon was seen to contribute to both, and to form part of a routine designed to maintain both:

> It's taken me probably about a year to get my head round. Well, to juggle and balance my time well enough that I am not absolutely knackered at the end of the day and just want to go home and drink a bottle of wine and go to bed. Now I just feel like, well no. Since I've taken steps to look after my health a bit better, eat a bit better, and take time out like the massage things, it just seems like my energy levels have gone up and life just seems a bit more manageable again.
>
> (Joanne)

Both of these examples illustrate how use of health treatments in the beauty salon are affected by changing life circumstances. In Chapter 3 I discussed the concept of time in triggering use of the beauty salon. The use of salons varies over the lifecourse and important life events are key factors in a client's decision to make use of the services of a beauty therapist. These events may be welcomed (e.g. a marriage or pregnancy) but to some extent are perceived as traumatic by the woman. This 'stress' is coped with by recourse to salon treatments. Therapists too saw their treatments in this way, and was one area of their business which was predicted to expand:

I: Are there any other changes that you think there will be in five years' time?

Charlotte (BT):   I think people will see massage, like, it's part of their health – it's not a luxury. It's something that people will think 'well I need it'. Because of the stress and the amount of people that are working on computers there has inevitably been more neck and head problems so people are going to love massage, so they can be fitting it into their lifestyle. Like, I don't want to keep going on about it but Americans see massage as an important part of their life. They have the massage therapist that comes to them once a week or once a month. It's their time for themselves and they will make that time because they know they benefit from it instead of it being a luxury.

Charlotte sees the merging of the two types of treatment area in the massage. Clients may have physical symptoms (neck and head pain) which result from work conditions, but they are also contributing to their own general sense of health. In this way massage becomes redefined. It is no longer seen as a luxury or an indulgence. Rather, it is viewed as an essential part of a healthy lifestyle.

The therapists also saw their knowledge and expertise as feeding into client health choices:

> We are doing body treatments. We do a lot of nutrition. So we are quite knowledgeable on knowing how to promote good health. We get a lot of people asking us, and we try to advise them on any treatment about how to back it up at home with doing certain things to promote good health, to make them healthier, advising them about nutrition and the water content, about exercise, about cutting out various toxins they are putting into themselves.
>
> (Alice BT)

Although both related to health, the ways in which treatments are described by clients differ between those with and those without the symptoms of chronic illness. Of course, those women who use salon treatments to alleviate the symptoms of illness also claim that this adds to their general sense of well-being. In fact it could be argued that the beauty salon is one area where treatment and diagnosis transcend the mind/body dualism prevalent in bio-medical approaches. However, the motivation for attending the salon differs between the two groups of clients. These women appear to be operating with differing definitions of health, and also different health priorities. The clients suffering from medically recognised illnesses are focused around improving their condition through alleviation of physical symptoms. They did not speak of obtaining health, but rather were concerned with avoiding pain and discomfort. This is able to co-exist with more holistic notions of health, but this is not the priority. For this reason Sandra, who attended the beauty salon for treatment of her MS, also enjoyed manicures and other beauty treatments. However, these were not seen as beneficial to her health in the same way, but as able to 'cheer you up and make you feel a bit better', which contributed to an overall positive feeling. However her priority remained the alleviation of physical symptoms. This approach chimes with Blaxter's finding that those who are coping with a chronic condition and managing the symptoms may reject negative definitions of health as the absence of illness, rather seeing themselves as 'healthy' in lay terms when their symptoms are minimal (Blaxter, 1990).

In contrast, the women who did not exhibit specific symptoms of illness or disease were concerned to capitalise on their physical state through investment in their health and the storage of bodily capital (Bourdieu, 1984, 1990). In this sense the body was used as a marker of other social and cultural factors related to well-being in its broadest sense. For example, as Joanne explains, her use of massage is integral to a body programme which regulates her intake of food, alcohol, and levels of exercise. She has been prompted to undertake these initiatives by increasing responsibility at work and her inability to cope with the demands of her job if her physical and emotional well-being are not regarded as a priority and managed as such. The upward mobility in her promotion within a highly pressurised service sector job has also caused anxiety:

> I started [work] very new. I really leapt from a team member who could just sort of sink into the background to a job

with a lot more responsibility where I am the only person who does what I do. If I'm not there it doesn't get done.

Joanne's cared-for or 'disciplined' body displays her acceptance and internalisation of disciplinary practices beneficial to success at work. It also displays her successful attainment of a particular form of middle-class heterosexual femininity. Although Blaxter does not put forward these arguments, this type of lay definition is comparable to those in her study who defined health in terms of a healthy lifestyle. This view was particularly apparent among the young. She also found that women were more likely than men to include their ability to maintain social relationships and responsibilities as important to their view of health (Blaxter, 1990). Both of these definitions were expressed by the women in this study who described their beauty salon visits in terms of health and well-being. The individual responsibility for well-being is therefore yet another demand placed upon salon clients and one which they use salon treatments to manage.

Producing health in the salon

What the evidence from beauty salon clients in relation to health shows us is that the medicalisation thesis which I outlined above does not stand up to scrutiny. Although some elements of the Foucauldian approach are useful, in themselves they cannot provide an explanation of the patterned nature of heath-related behaviours. I have explained this in terms of the healthy lifestyle, and understood this in relation to specific social positions. We are also witnessing an increasing commodification of the body. The body has become both a site for the display of identity and capitals, and as such is a driver of consumption. It is also used as a symbol in marketing, advertising, and increasingly in business, to display a particular image. It is in this sense that disciplinary practices operate upon and through the body. As I pointed out in relation to employment, the intensification of the commodification of men's bodies is one of the factors prompting men's increasing use of salons.

It is crucial here to maintain the link between bodies and com-modification, as this allows us to discuss wider structural factors and to understand how the bodies of different people are produced and read in very different ways. I have been careful to stress this differentially experienced body throughout this book, and have also emphasised how the practices carried out in the salon are accessed by different groups of clients for reasons which tie in with social relationships that lie outside the salon doors. Health-related treatments are no different.

In the UK, the political discourse of the liberal free market economy has intensified since the early 1980s. This has contributed to the shifting of responsibility from wider social provision to the individual (Nettleton, 1997). At the time of writing the UK government has proposed that patients who smoke may be asked to sign a contract agreeing to give up, and to improve their health status. Failure to conform to this contract would result in a fine. Chronic heart disease would also be managed by a change in lifestyle which is the responsibility of the individual (Meikle, 2003). Although the reaction to these proposals has been generally negative, the very fact that such an idea is being considered illus-trates how far individual responsibility has pervaded health care thinking. Lupton has outlined how public health initiatives have moved away from a focus upon the social group, or the social environment as a source of illness, towards viewing the individual as responsible for their own health and well-being (Lupton, 1994). Coupled with this, the characteristics of a new 'surveillance medicine' mean that while health is the responsibility of the individual, risk is assessed through monitoring of non-ill, healthy populations (Armstrong, 1995). This process has been taken up by beauty salon clients, but is differentially experienced according to their physical state. Thus the woman with a chronic condition (who enjoys a level of disposable income) no longer relies solely on public health provision but instead pays for health care through a relatively accessible commercial setting. The woman who is healthy maintains this state through preventive measures. Her understanding of a healthy state is tied to wider consumption practices.

The body as a project remains the focus of a more middle-class clientele in the salon, and, if we follow Savage *et al.* (1992), a particular segment of the middle class. These types of women focus on 'feeling treatments' in promoting a general sense of well-being. In this sense their definition of health, and their experience of their bodies, is mediated through the lens of their class position. This approach to the body as project appears to be a widening phenomenon in contemporary Western societies (Bourdieu, 1984; Featherstone, 1991; Witz, 2000), and has been linked by Featherstone to the expansion of the new petit bourgeoisie:

> If we turn to the new petit bourgeois habitus it is clear that whereas the bourgeois has a sense of ease and confidence in his body, the petit bourgeois is uneasy with his body, constantly self-consciously checking, watching and correcting himself. Hence the attraction of body maintenance techniques, the new Californian sports and forms of exercise, cosmetics, health food, where the body is treated as a sign for others and not as an instrument.
>
> (Featherstone, 1991, p. 90)

However, for women the body 'always, already' acts as a vital form of capital. Work on the body is necessary for the achievement of an 'appropriate' femininity. As Skeggs (1997) has also pointed out, the body may be one resource invested in by working-class women where access to other forms of capital (e.g. education, economic) is limited. However, the form that this investment takes varies among the women attending the salon. All invest in bodily capital, but for some this is converted into other forms of usable capital, while for others it is simply a means of 'putting a floor under' their relative social position or a way of achieving a state of 'normality' (Skeggs, 1997). In terms of investment in femininity as a strategy to gain limited rewards but avoid sanction, corrective treatments such as removal of facial hair are vital. However, health-related treatments are linked in different ways to femininity and class.

The location where treatments are offered is important here. In this study Yvette's place, the salon most aimed at a white working-class clientele, offered very little in the way of 'feeling treatments', and staff there were adamant that their clientele were not interested in paying relatively large sums for treatments where no immediate result was visible. However, in salons catering to a more middle-class clientele, treatments related to well-being were in high demand. It may be that treatments are allied to class not only in terms of cost, but also in relation to context. For example, Pirie (2003) shows that where working-class women were offered Shiatsu treatments in a GP surgery there was a high degree of take-up and a positive response to the initiative. The cost element here was removed and the need to venture into a potentially unfamiliar environment to experience a treatment not regarded as a necessity was also overcome.

All of these trends taken together help us to more fully understand the concept of lifestyle in relation to health. It is a concept based on consumption and display. Either conspicuous consumption or bodily discipline form key elements of any particular lifestyle, and this varies according to social position. The healthy lifestyle incorporates not only ideas about health or the absence of illness, but also a wider notion of body work and responsibility for health status. It also allows the symbols of health to be read in a social rather than a purely bio-medical form. For example, we can look healthy either through attention to diet and exercise or through the application of a particular style of make-up. By linking together a wide range of behaviours under the umbrella of 'lifestyle' we should be careful about our use of language. I intend not to fall for the language used by marketeers or to subscribe to an individual involved in a project of self-creation. Rather I wish to use it to allow the incorporation of social factors, including the commodified body, into understandings of health.

Accessing salon treatments and the justificatory discourses used also ties in with the reasons why clients make their first visits to the salon, and in turn this is dependent on what I have termed 'self-view' and worldview' (or habitus). I discuss this concept more fully in Chapter 3, but it is relevant to remember here that the impetus to beauty salon use is itself a complex process which requires the potential client to justify her salon use in terms which 'fit' with her self-image and personal beliefs. She must also hold a view of the salon which does not exclude 'people like her'. Health treatments provide two forms of justification for salon use – either as providing concrete physical results, or in terms of promoting a 'healthy lifestyle'.

I have outlined how client use of salons for health treatments may be understood, but how does the claim to care for health feature in the professional competencies of beauty therapists? In order to enhance their professional status beauty therapists claim to work on the body and on feelings. Both of these are seen to contribute to promoting health. Although there is some tension in the industry between specialists in different areas, all agree that they are concerned to make clients look better and feel better.

'We deal with healthy bodies': the professional claims of beauty therapists

Defining a profession is contentious. It may be done from within a variety of theoretical frameworks and I have discussed this in more detail in Chapter 4. Although it is beyond the scope of this research to enter into a detailed debate about the nature of beauty therapy as a profession, or in fact the defining principles of professions *per se*, it is interesting to note how the claims to professional status made by beauty therapists often centre around their health-promoting skills. I am not operating here with any particular rigid definition of a profession, but am interested in understanding how the therapists themselves described their work.

Beauty therapists are aware of the low status of the occupation, and also the ambivalence and curiosity aroused by their profession. Although trained as professionals, public perceptions of therapists do not always match this aspiration. The image of the profession has changed in recent years as client numbers increase and beauty therapy enjoys a higher press profile. The client base has extended through new treatments coming under the rubric of beauty therapy, and from new clients attending salons. However, as I have described above, a division exists in the profession between those who wish to emphasise the 'beauty' side of their work and those who wish to be known primarily as 'therapists'. The following teacher of beauty therapy illustrates these disagreements in her own college:

> Personally, I don't like the term beauty therapy. We were discussing this in the staff meeting and all the beauty therapy advisers that we have, they have salons, all wanted us to keep the name beauty therapy. But the complementary students, the ones doing reflexology, massage, aromatherapy, exercise, they don't like 'beauty therapy'. And so we've got the pressure from them to change it because they don't want to be associated with 'beauty' because they think it's something different. And they are something different, it's just that we offer it through the beauty therapy department.
>
> (Sue BT)

This division rests upon the twin pressures of economics and professional status. Some argue that 'beauty' should be dropped from the title of the profession in order to raise professional status and to emphasise the types of treatments carried out which have little to do with appearance. Others argue that as the majority of clients visit the salon for 'beauty' treatments it would be commercially irresponsible to downplay this side of their work. All therapists are trained in a wide range of treatments, but if possible prefer to specialise in one area. Those who enjoy massage, aromatherapy and reflexology regard their professional expertise as contributing to a holistic sense of well-being in the client. They are less concerned with appearance and more concerned that the client should feel good. Other therapists find massage 'boring' or tiring:

> What I don't like is massage. It's so boring. . . . You don't really need to think about anything. The client is half-asleep and you're getting along with whatever area you are supposed to be massaging and it can get quite boring, you know, a whole

hour. With waxing you can talk and the time goes by so quickly.

(Wendy BT)

During massage treatments the therapist must use the whole of her body to apply the correct pressure. This can be tiring on a long-term basis. Massage treatments also entail minimal conversation with clients, and those therapists who preferred 'looking treatments' missed this side of their work. In this case, although therapists are always concerned that their clients should feel good, a priority is that the client should also look better after a treatment. This specialisation is reflected in the preferences of clients who prefer either 'feeling treatments' or 'looking treatments'. Despite this specialisation all therapists view themselves as part of the same industry with some contribution to make to improving the overall sense of well-being among their clients. The looking versus feeling distinction can be maintained to a certain extent by assessing the preferred specialisms of therapists and the types of treatments clients choose. However, even looking treatments are seen to contribute to health in a psychological sense. In a highly visual culture, looking good is read as an indicator of health. The external body is read increasingly as a signifier of an inner state of being. This is one of the reasons why clients who access looking treatments also describe the psychological boost that they receive on being able to 'hold their head high' when they leave the salon.

Beauty therapy training includes knowledge of human biology, information on the use of chemicals and any contra-indications which may occur, some level of business knowledge and accounting, and so on. It is striking that every beauty therapist interviewed compared herself to a nurse either in terms of training, aptitude or type of work carried out:

The beauty therapist who undergoes two years' training is on the same path as a nurse. All right, they are not medics and they don't have the responsibility of dealing out drugs, but they do a lot of theory training. They've got a lot of assignments and assessments to get through. So the training is as rigorous as nursing training.

(Kirsty BT)

Some described how ambitions for a nursing career, or in Kirsty's case the desire to train as a doctor, had been thwarted. Kirsty compared her knowledge in some areas to that of a GP:

> My daughter goes to school where there are a lot of medics and doctors and every now and then we get into arguments over the standards, what we know and what we don't know, what we're supposed to know. As far as I'm aware a GP gets six weeks' training on the skin. Obviously we are not doctors, we would never claim to be doctors. We deal with healthy bodies instead of unhealthy bodies, but we're training on the skin for two years.

(Kirsty BT)

The beauty therapists in this study were obviously keen to compare their training and expertise to that of other medical professionals. This is done primarily to boost their claims to a professional status. It is perhaps most valid in relation to the health treatments received by clients, particularly in relation to the alleviation of symptoms of illnesses such as MS and RSI. However, the beauty therapists also acknowledge key differences in their work in that they 'deal with healthy bodies'. In this sense they operate with definitions of health which emphasise well-being rather than a strictly bio-medical model. This mirrors the lay beliefs held by their clients. Rather than specialising in the treatment of sick bodies, the beauty therapist is skilled in preserving and boosting the health status of her non-ill clients.

Therapists themselves also claim to fulfil a counselling function in their work. This attention to the mind along with the body is one key element of lay definitions of health which bio-medical health professionals, particularly in a public health setting, are increasingly unable to cater for. Beauty therapists pay attention to emotions at the same time as working on the body. Psychological, emotional and physical health are not separated fully in any of the treatments received. This counselling function has positive benefits for the client, and both positive and negative effects for the therapist. While she may gain satisfaction from allowing the client to leave the salon unburdened and happier, the emotional toll this takes can also be damaging for her own physical and emotional health:

> I would say 80 per cent of my clients, maybe higher, have problems that they tell me about every time they come in. . . . They come back because they feel cared for. They come back because you will listen to them whereas at home you know the husband will say 'God if you talk about that once more I will scream', but they pay you to listen as well you see, as well as having the treatment. I have clients here, they'll pay forty pounds for a facial and they're lying there the whole time with their eyes open instead of relaxing and going right into it, they're lying there the whole time and telling me about their latest trauma, and I'm thinking 'what are you getting from this facial'? But what they're getting from the facial is unburdening of their problems.
>
> (Colette BT)

This emotional labour is an ambivalent resource. It plays a significant part in the therapist's claims to professional status and job satisfaction. These skills are also highly feminised and as such are seen as part of what women do 'naturally' anyway. By emphasising this element of her work the therapist risks devaluing the very skills which she claims actually elevate her standing.

In claiming to work with the physical body, to provide psychological counselling, and to engage in an intimate body relationship which improves emotional health, therapists are laying claim to a number of roles which cut across occupations within the health professions. This is one of the strengths of beauty therapy. However, it is part of beauty therapy ethics that all therapists know their own limitations in terms of their knowledge and training, and where appropriate referrals to other specialists are made. This is sometimes to the detriment of their own economic gain. Kirsty describes how a regular client attended for a treatment but 'she came in one day and she just didn't look right'. The client complained of a headache and the therapist refused to treat her, instead recommending that she visit a doctor. The client became angry:

> She got upset with me, I was there to treat her, she was paying me to treat her, regardless of the fact that in my professional opinion it wasn't right to go ahead with the treatment and she stormed out. . . . And that was it, I'd lost a client.
>
> (Kirsty BT)

It later transpired that on the insistence of her husband the woman did visit a hospital and collapsed in the waiting room with an aneurysm on the brain. This story is told to emphasise the professional ethics and competency of the beauty therapist which are seen to override financial gain. However, it is also clear that the accurate and timely referral to the medical profession also boosts the health-related claims of the therapist at the same time as differentiating their expertise.

The relationship with the medical profession

Receiving treatment from a beauty therapist for the alleviation of symptoms of illness or chronic conditions met with a mixed response from medical practitioners. Some clients were registered with GPs who offered a wide range of non bio-medical treatments in their practices. Others remained sceptical about the long-term health benefits of massage, aromatherapy or other complementary therapies. Relationships with other areas of the medical profession appear to have altered over time, and to be developing:

> We have had quite a lot of opposition from the nursing and medical professions but we've overcome that. Also from the massage therapy side, that's increasing a lot and initially we had a lot of opposition from physiotherapists but now their role has changed, and the fact that they're doing a lot of diag-

nostic work and also using a lot more equipment, and they are now bringing in massage therapists to help them with the straightforward massage treatments.

(Emily BT)

It would be a mistake to simply emphasise the benefits gained by therapists in their association with the medical profession. As they pointed out, there are also some benefits which operate in the opposite direction. For example, in the early 1990s under the Conservative government in the UK, GP surgeries became fund holders. This meant that, in largely controlling its own budgets, the practice was able to buy in services considered appropriate for its patients:

> They [GPs] discovered that there were quite a lot of things that they could do within their surgeries which people wanted which actually brought them revenue. Things like, you know, removing moles and doing varicose veins. . . . So I think they sort of discovered that there was quite a lot of treatments if you like, marked 'beauty' that they were capable of doing, and if they wanted to increase that side of the business for extra revenue then they had to link in actually with beauty salons, because that's where the public went and asked about these problems.

(Emily BT)

Although the funding for GPs in the UK has now changed, this association may continue to have benefits in the future:

> I think you're going to see much more a cross-over as we said earlier between medical, para-medical, beauty, because medics who are interested in cosmetic treatments realise that the way to get clients is through beauty salons.

(Kirsty BT)

It was not unknown for therapists to treat clients on a GP recommendation, but there was little evidence of any formal referral system. Beauty therapists generally welcomed the recommendations and saw it as evidence of their own professional status as well as their contributions to the health of the client. However, occasional examples did arise where the recommendation was seen to be inappropriate and unwelcome:

> A GP actually sent somebody to me a couple of weeks ago with what looked to me like a bit of a cyst on her forehead. I was flabbergasted that a GP would send this person, said, 'A beauty therapist could sort that out for you'. I said, 'Oh, no, we are not medically trained, we can do skin tags and, you know, thread veins and stuff like that. We are not trained to remove something like that.' But she said, 'My GP sent me' [laughs]. I said, 'you will have to go back to him.'
>
> (Alice BT)

Here, the ethical imperative of knowing the limits of their own professional competencies and responsibilities was challenged by the actions of the doctor. This referral of the patient was regarded as unprofessional by Alice. The fact that she was 'flabbergasted' illustrates that this kind of overstepping the boundaries between beauty therapy and bio-medicine did not occur on a regular basis and that, although the relationship between the two spheres is dynamic and sometimes conflicting, there does appear to be an understanding in both professions of the appropriate role of each.

The salon generally relies much more on client self-referral than on professional referral (Freidson, 1970). This means that the beauty therapist is dependent for her business on the lay understandings of her clients and their cultural location which means that they are, or are not, likely to purchase her services. Word of mouth is important in recruiting clients. In this type of system the professional knowledge of the therapist, although important, must be tempered by her relationship to clients. They arrive with their own culturally dependent expectations, and demand a service suitable for their needs. This of course creates a tension between the beauty therapist as professional expert, and the therapist as service sector worker. When discussing clients who are less than polite, or who question her professional qualifications, Diane describes succinctly the ambiguity of her reaction:

> So you have to, not in a rude way, but you just have to be a bit direct, do you know what I mean? But you're in a service industry so what do you do? Do you say, 'Bugger off you old cow'? Or do you have to be a bit sort of two-faced or subservient to do the treatment?
>
> (Diane BT)

Beauty therapists also experience the tension between their claims to health-promoting status and the need to make a profit for the business within which they work:

> [After talking about how clients relax during treatment]
> And I think that is why we might be better at retailing because they [client] have just had this wonderful treatment and then they are more in the frame of mind to buy. They think, 'Oh I can extend that' and I can take a bit of this salon, this treatment home with me.
>
> (Sue BT)

In contrast, medical professionals are not placed in a self-referral situation to their patients. Their knowledge and expertise are more protected, and also less familiar to clients. Within this type of profession, regulation is dependent on colleagues rather than lay perceptions. Referrals are formal. More often than not the patient defers to the specialised and professional competencies of the practitioner.

Because of this, beauty therapists must be sure to offer what the client requires, rather than conform to the needs of health professionals, despite the fact that it is precisely this association with the health profession which boosts their status. Beauty therapists may be brought into the health service but are most welcome for their input into improving the general sense of well-being for the patient, rather than any acknowledgement on the part of the medical profession that beauty therapists are able to carry out medicalised treatments. However, this suspicion from the medical establishment does not prevent clients themselves from using the salon for treatment of medical conditions.

The beauty therapist boosts her professional status by emphasising her contribution to health care practices and her good working relationship with the medical profession:

> I mean this industry, we are working alongside the medical field and I believe that's where the industry should go. . . . I work in conjunction with the doctors in the area. I've got a number of instances that have happened with clients of mine who've been to the doctors because of things I've done or said, and the doctor has made a positive comment on that. The doctors I work with trust me, they refer people to me, that's what we need.
>
> (Kirsty BT)

This may be seen as an example of professional rhetoric (Fine, 1996). However, it seems that no *formal* client referral system from traditional medical services to the therapist is on the horizon. Rather, therapists may refer their clients to medical facilities.

The relationship with complementary therapies

Beauty therapists then might be compared more usefully to other complementary therapists rather than to traditional medical practitioners. Turning to a non-biomedical practitioner for treatment of chronic conditions is a trend also influencing the growth of complementary therapies. It is to some extent due to the success of bio-medicine in prolonging life expectancy and treating non-chronic conditions (Sharma, 1994). As longevity and health become the expectation, then those experiencing illness which cannot be 'cured' in the traditional sense may lose faith in traditional medicine and seek out the expertise of those, such as the beauty therapist, who are also able to pay attention to the social aspects of illness. Trust is also a vital basis to relationships between professionals and their clients. Although trust in doctors, and especially nurses, remains high in the UK, a number of recent scandals centring around the conduct of the medical profession have undermined this confidence (Allsop and Saks, 2002). The decline in unquestioning trust in experts is also a characteristic which has been identified across the professions in industrial societies (Beck, 1992).

Both beauty therapy and complementary therapies have faced a similar dilemma around claims to professional status and the relationship with bio-medicine. At the heart of this dilemma lies the legitimate claims to qualifications, expertise and knowledge. For example, homeopathy in the UK does want to make claims about diagnosis and treatment of specific conditions, while other complementary therapies have been reluctant to make these claims (Cant and Sharma, 1995, 1996). The professional project engaged in by homeopaths has brought them closer to the status of medics and into a more congenial relationship with bio-medicine. In contrast, reflexologists have avoided this level of engagement in order to maintain their own sets of professional ethics and values. However, as yet, other complementary therapies enjoy a closer relationship with the medical profession than does beauty therapy. The future route that this relationship will take is one of the causes of disagreement in the industry around the relative value of clinicising the salon.

It is likely that, at most, beauty therapists will take on a role similar to occupational therapists, osteopaths or some of the complementary therapists more recognised by the medical profession, although with very different expertise and levels of training. Beauty therapists are unlikely to be involved in treatment decisions, but will have specific treatments delegated to them by bio-medical practitioners. Despite the thwarted medical ambitions of some, most would appear to be happy with this relationship. Clients will also self-refer in order to treat medically diagnosed conditions. This self-referral may entail rejection of, or dissatisfaction with, the medical profession. It may also be viewed in relation to a treatment package which contains elements of both. Similarly, visits to the beauty salon are viewed with varying amounts of approval in the wider medical sphere. Where beauty therapy really comes into its own, however, is in contributing to wider concepts of health and well-being. The rapid expansion of the client base and the amount of business generated in recent years may be viewed in relation to this role. The increasing likelihood for women and men to visit complementary therapists and to engage in preventive health measures has strengthened the professional status of the beauty therapist. As such her relationship with the medical profession and other complementary therapies has increased in significance.

In the salon we can see that what might loosely be termed 'medicine' is being delivered in a non-medical setting. This affects the ways in which treatments are viewed, and also the power relationships between practitioner and client. In the GP surgery or hospital the qualified health professional occupies a powerful position which is bolstered by public ignorance of medical procedures, by the qualifications held by the medic, and by the setting itself. The identity of the privileged male doctor also reinforces this unequal power relation (Witz, 1992). However, when health-related treatments are carried out in a community setting, this relationship is unbalanced. In the beauty salon, the client faces someone who is less formally qualified and is employed in a feminised, low-status, service industry. The client is also paying for the services. This in itself means that where disposable income is available, treatments in the salon are likely to be accessed to improve health.

Does a visit to the beauty salon promote health?

Throughout my research I have emphasised the fact that the world of the beauty salon is not to be understood simply by reference to beauty. The practices and discourses intersecting in the world of the salon are complex and ambiguous. The beauty therapist engages in a range of different practices, and even though all therapists recognise themselves as belonging to a similar industry, there are a wide range of specialisms subsumed under this umbrella profession. Here I have focused on the health-related aspects of the beauty therapist's work. However, it could be claimed that all activities in the salon contribute to the health of the client in that they reinforce feelings of well-being. The beauty salon may be one of the spaces where it is possible to transcend the mind/body dualism inherent in much of Western medicine (in fact in much of Western thought generally). The therapists contribute to looking good and feeling good, and although it is possible to go some way to separating out particular treatments which fall on each side of the divide, both therapists and clients also argue that all treatments contribute to both.

The growth in the popularity of the beauty salon (and to some extent complementary therapies) is linked to the increasing investment in body projects at the same time as trust in medical professionals is declining. Commodification of the body is also inherent in these body projects (Featherstone, 1982). (If the creation of the 'appropriate' body becomes a priority then it seems logical that in a capitalist economy, businesses will appear to service this growing market.) Turner has gone so far as to argue that contemporary Western society may be termed the 'somatic society' in that the 'major political and personal problems are both problematized in the body and expressed through it' (Turner, 1996, p. 1).

I have shown how even health may be understood in terms of these wider transformations, and how the beauty salon is one space where definitions and experiences of health are being negotiated and produced. Of course healthy can only ever be healthy in relation to what is 'normal', and normality makes sense only in reference to specific social positioning in terms of class, age, gender, ethnicity and sexuality. The way that widening definitions of health and an increased investment in projects of the body are being taken up by different groups of people may be illustrated by investigating health treatments in the beauty salon.

Despite the WHO defining health as a complete state of physical, mental and social well-being, this seems to be an unrealistic aim. In fact it is difficult to imagine anyone maintaining such a state in perpetuity. Like happiness, this definition describes health as something to be sought and enjoyed fleetingly, often being appreciated in retrospect when ill-health or unhappiness begins. Instead it might be more realistic and analytically useful to see health as a relationship between biology, social relationships and 'lifestyle'. The balance between these elements will vary between populations, individuals and over time. Beauty therapy clients access health treatments in the salon for all three reasons. Attention to their physical state is a priority for some and a by-product for others. Social relationships are fostered in the counselling role fulfilled by therapists. The well-being produced in the salon also facilitates an improvement in the social relationships clients experience outside the salon. The relaxing feeling produced by some treatments, the time for escapism, or the achievement of a desired physical outcome promotes what might be termed social health for the client. It is in the area of 'lifestyle' that the commodification of the body becomes most relevant. Clients are not only purchasing the services of a therapist in a commercial transaction, they are also investing in bodily capital through the expenditure of economic capital. They are engaged in a consumption process at the same time as they are contributing to their state of well-being. Therapists too are caught between emphasising their health-related credentials, their employment in a service industry, and the need to make money in a commercial setting. For both clients and therapists a move away from purely bio-medical understandings of health is necessary to make sense of the practices in the beauty salon.

Chapter 6

'You feel better when you leave'

Some concluding comments

I: Do you think it [beauty salon use] is a positive thing in your life then?

Bridget: Yes, probably because it makes me feel better. I don't go there to be squeezed and tucked and pinched with the hope that one day I might look like Christy Brinkley or something like that. I just like shutting my eyes for half an hour while somebody messes around so you feel better when you leave. It's nice to have that little bit of attention.

I have enjoyed the time spent in beauty salons. I have also enjoyed the treatments I have received there, although this enjoyment has been tempered by a researcher's eye. Some of the treatment experiences have been relaxing, rejuvenating episodes in my life. Others have verged on the ridiculous. On one occasion as I lay on my back with my legs pulled up and a young woman I had never met before applied hot wax to my thighs only to remove it painfully seconds later, the full impact of the beauty industry became apparent. What powerful force could have persuaded me of the need to undergo such a procedure, while at the same time breaking every rule of polite social engagement? Perhaps only something connected to the intimacies and uncertainties of the body could have placed me, and millions of other women, in such a ridiculous position.

The beauty industry as we understand it today is a comparatively recent historical product. While both men and women have always paid attention to their dress and their bodies, in the past a com-modified mass market for beauty products and services did not exist. In the USA, the origins of the beauty salon lay with women entrepreneurs providing services in an informal setting. Particularly for black women in the USA, the beauty salon has played an impor-tant role in local community solidarity and political activities. The impetus for a mass market in beauty products came with the growth of urban centres, and developments in technology which allowed the production and distribution of products on a large scale. Improvements in street lighting, the development of the department store and the growth of the cinema also played their part. However, it is only since the Second World War that the 'beauty system' described by Wolf (1990) came into existence.

Partly due to this fragmented history, the salon exists in a variety of formats around the world, and offers myriad experiences. In this study I have categorised the various treatment types as: health treat-ments; pampering; routine grooming; and corrective treatments. Therapists also claim to fulfil a counselling role for their clients. It is possible to visit the salon in embarrassment and secrecy to have facial hair removed. It is also possible to invest in a massage as part of a health care regime, or to enjoy the camaraderie of other clients while receiving a manicure. No one arrives in the beauty salon purely as a result of accident or chance. The context of the first visit is important in understanding the role salon treatments play in the lives of clients. 'Getting in' to the salon involves an understanding of biographical factors, the development of the life-course, and the habitus of the potential client. Discourses around the 'doing' of gender in any particular society in a specific historical time period will also impact on this process. Potential clients must feel that salons are places for 'people like them', and their visits must fit within their worldview and self-view. This categorisation is a reworking of Bourdieu's concept of the habitus (Bourdieu, 1990; Crossley, 2001). Time is important here in that lives unfold over time, and the amount and quality of time available to the client varies during the lifecourse. In addition, the claim for 'time for myself' is one which may be understood in terms of competing demands on women's lives. Time spent in the salon is a statement of personal value and a means of coping with the variety of roles and pressures experienced by the women in this study. There is much space for the politics of time to enter the discussion here. What has been termed the political economy of time has become a large and interesting debate encompassing work life balance, demands around employment conditions, and the need for well-funded and regulated childcare (Southerton *et al.*, 2001; Fagan 2002). In addition, as Storr (2003) points out, the expectation of time to spend on personal enjoyment has become a common discourse in the lives of women. This individualised coping mechanism finds echoes in salon use by clients.

Once the client begins her visits to the salon her sense of appropriateness guides its use. Appropriateness is an all-encompassing concept which involves the negotiation of gender, class, ethnicity and sexuality into identity. Appropriateness involves knowledge, skill and performance. Knowing how to 'make the best of yourself', often heard in beauty salons, is a glib phrase which disguises a large amount of complex knowledge. Beauty therapists may guide clients in their selection of treatments, or recommend products to them. The popular media, TV make-over shows and advertising are all sources of information on what is and is not appropriate for particular types of men and women to wear, to purchase, even how and what to eat. In addition, social relationships reinforce consumption patterns and choices in style. In the very process of growing up female, a woman will learn how to police the boundaries of her own looking and being a woman.

Knowledge is transformed into skill in producing the bodily dispositions of identity. Learning how to wash, condition and style hair, or to cleanse, tone and moisturise skin, involves knowledge of product types and how to combine them, as well as the skills to apply them. Where salon clients do not feel that they have the skills to achieve the desired results then the services of the professional beauty therapist are called in. Eyebrow shaping, eyelash dyeing, manicures, facials and waxing are examples of treatments which could be carried out by women in their own homes, but are instead purchased from therapists due to the level of skill required to avoid pain or messy results. For the therapist this type of skill is a contradictory asset. On the one hand, she derives much of her business from these areas. On the other hand, as such skills often remain unrecognised, being seen as something women inherently know how to do anyway, therapists are unable to base their clams to professional status on these skills.

As well as knowledge and skill, appropriateness requires performance. Performance is a vital aspect of gender identity in that it demonstrates the achievement of appropriateness. Performance in this sense should not be viewed as a voluntaristic act, but rather as a set of conscious choices, and unconscious dispositions. The taken for grantedness of posture, speech patterns, or taste in consumer goods are all aspects of performance in the sense I have used it. For the beauty salon clients in this study, treatments received helped to achieve a type of bodily being with which they felt comfortable. For Bourdieu, this comfort arises from the alignment of the habitus with objective social structures. The limitations of opportunity produced by social location result in tastes and preferences which come to be seen as choices. Gendered performance here is a result of position taking by the woman, which is itself allied closely to social position (Bourdieu, 1998, 2001). I have attempted to avoid the over-determinism of this close alignment in my concept of appropriateness, partly through breaking it down into knowledge, skill and performance, and by investigating appropriateness in a variety of social and geographical spaces. In particular I have discussed the salon space; exercise spaces; work spaces; private spaces; going out spaces; and 'empty spaces' which refers to questions of sexuality not directly addressed in interviews.

I have found Bourdieu's work useful in making sense of empirical material, although I have also expressed reservations about his conceptual schema, not least in relation to his understanding of gender. Within a broad framework it is possible to understand all salon visits as an investment in bodily capital. For women, bodily capital is an available capital, if one of limited value. It may be traded in limited circumstances, but will not ensure the rewards inherent in other types of capital, such as education. There is also the added danger that bodily capital may go unrecognised, and as such remain unrewarded. However, sanctions are attached if the borders of an 'acceptable' appearance are breached.

A woman negotiates her relationship to femininity from within the particular position of her own life. Bourdieu refers to the imposition of femininity upon women as *symbolic violence*, and for him it is an imperceptible process, almost fully successful in the way that female habitus and female social position become aligned (Bourdieu, 2001). What the fragmentation of discourses and practices in the salon suggests, however, is that different women invest in their femininity in different arenas, and that femininity itself is produced in a variety of different social institutions. The woman is constantly moving through these spaces and juggling her own experiences and levels of commitment within them. This allows the potential for ambiguity, contradiction and critique. In making use of the term 'femininity' to apply across these spaces I am aware of potential criticism:

> Using the concept of femininity to apply to all women is to misuse a historically specific representation. It was produced in power relations, in the interests of particular groups, invested in by other groups and it cannot therefore . . . be applied to all women.
>
> (Skeggs, 1997, p. 21)

Femininity in this sense has no place in a discussion of women's beauty practices. There is no ahistorical, depoliticised ideal which can be applied to all women. Instead, I have used femininity to relate to the practices, identities and representations of what it means to be a 'woman' in any given society in a particular historical period. Skeggs is correct to be wary of the label, yet she herself outlines its use as a yardstick against which the white working-class women in her study were measured and found lacking. However, I have also argued that in researching body practices we can at times, and very carefully, speak of practices which have resonance for women *per se*. The clearest example of this is the presence of facial hair, which was viewed in this study as a signifier of masculinity. However, I am also aware that the women in this study were all invested to some extent in the trappings of hetero-sexual femininity. The very nature of the sample means that all had attended a beauty salon, or had worked in one. Even among these women there was an ambivalence at the heart of their relationship with femininity. I have encapsulated this ambiguity in the concept of appropriateness.

The labour involved in producing the gendered body is exten-sive. One of the issues which this research highlights is the myth-ology of the 'natural' body. This labour may be understood in terms of the work carried out by the professional beauty therapist; the everyday practices invested in by beauty salon clients; and the role of beauty treatments in the work lives of clients. Beauty thera-pists are not part of a high-status occupation and are aware of the negative associations of their work. These negative associations arise for several reasons. Beauty therapists are employed in a feminised industry with an overwhelmingly female clientele. Their work is closely associated with the body in a way which is open to misinterpretation. All the therapists interviewed were wary of being viewed as sex workers. Their qualification structure is widely misunderstood and they are often regarded as 'bimbos' with little intelligence and minimal formal training. They also work at the intersection of the service sector and a commercial enterprise, and pay and conditions in the industry are generally poor. For all these reasons, beauty therapists may be defensive about their chosen occupation, and feel the need to reinforce their professional expertise. One of the key problems in claiming professional status is that the skills possessed by beauty therapists, and those used most regularly in the pursuit of their work, are those seen to be inherent in a feminine identity. Beauty therapists claim that they offer a counselling service to clients, and that they must learn to manage sometimes difficult and intimate social encounters. This aspect of their work can be emotionally and physically draining, but it is also fulfilling. However, this emotional labour is not a skill which is generally recognised and rewarded, particularly when performed by women. The ability to manage feelings in this way is a skill which is learned during practice, but is not formally addressed to any great extent during training. Therapists and trainers are more likely to view these skills as being a result of personality and aptitude. This places the individual therapist and the profession more widely in a difficult position. If women are seen as inherently possessing highly developed interpersonal skills, intuition and the ability to manage their own emotions and those of others, then it is difficult to formalise these skills into a recognisable set of professional competencies deserving reward.

The work lives of clients are also crucial to understanding the importance of the beauty salon. Grooming treatments for both men and women are geared towards appearance in the workplace. These routine visits are engaged in to obtain a level of appearance regarded as acceptable, and also sometimes to save time in preparing for work. The management of appearance in the workplace has become more carefully regulated by employers. Writers such as Adkins (2001) and Witz et al. (2003) argue that this may be understood in terms of an aestheticisation of the workplace. The bodies of workers in the service sector have become part of the resources of employers to the extent that bodily performances are now not only demanded, but also rewarded as career achievements. In this study, the beauty salon clients most closely regulated in their workplaces were those that came into closest contact with the public during the course of their employment. A key aspect of the aestheticisation argument is that particular performances or 'dispositions' (Witz et al., 2003) are more likely to be rewarded than others. In this way the female service sector worker faces a similar dilemma to the beauty therapist. Skills which are actually learned, and which require investment of time, money and effort, remain unrecognised when they are viewed as an immanent characteristic of femininity. The beauty salon then has become a service drawn on by workers in other service industries in order to produce a body which is required in the workplace. If we follow Adkins' arguments it seems that the male clients of salons are more likely to reap rewards for their investment than are female clients.

Beauty therapy can also be understood in relation to health in its broadest sense. Clients speak of the beneficial health effects of salon treatments in two key ways. First, some clients make use of treatments including massage, aromatherapy and reflexology in order to alleviate the symptoms of chronic illness such as Repetitive Strain Injury or Multiple Sclerosis. This group of clients manage their illness by using the therapist in conjunction with medical practitioners. Salon treatments in this sense are closely allied to the physical well-being of the client. In contrast, similar treatments may also contribute to a general sense of physical and mental well-being for non-ill clients. Health treatments in this second sense must be understood within a much broader framework. Claiming to be interested in the 'feeling' aspects of beauty treatments removes some of the stigma associated with 'looking treatments'. All clients and therapists were keen to avoid any accusations of vanity or charges of 'shallowness', which too close an association with appearance may elicit. In order to place health treatments in the context of clients' lives I have used explanations combining the physical, social relationships and lifestyle. The concept of the healthy lifestyle combines broad definitions of health with attention to social characteristics and consumption practices. I have used it to explain how women incorporate salon treatments into a style of life which regulates their food intake, exercise levels, alcohol consumption, grooming practices and leisure activities. Although these may seem tangentially related to health, for clients who viewed their health in holistic terms, these things were inseparable. The beauty salon may thus make some legitimate claims to be a health-promoting venue.

Beauty therapists boost their own professional status by favourable comparison of their role with that of medical practitioners. All the therapists compared themselves to nurses in the level of training they undergo and the detailed knowledge of human biology they possess. This association may be seen as a form of professional rhetoric (Fine, 1996), but also deserves to be taken seriously if we accept a holistic view of health rather than a narrow bio-medical definition. According to both client and therapist testimonies, salon treatments do contribute to the general social, mental and physical health of the client. There is also some evidence for a very informal referral system between health professionals and beauty therapists. However, some clients also spoke of a deep reluctance on the part of their GP to accept treatments in the salon as having any benefit whatsoever. It is perhaps more accurate to view the beauty therapist as a type of complementary therapist, engaged in a professional project which makes claims concerning levels of training and expertise, but which remains at some distance from bio-medicine.

The beauty salon is an important and fascinating world, and one which has increasingly received attention. Other aspects of the beauty industry have also come under careful scrutiny. Most useful studies are those which bridge the gap between detailed ethnography and theoretical interpretation (Furman, 1997; Rooks, 1998; Willett, 2000; Craig, 2002; Gimlin, 2002). All this work must grapple with the central issues of women's involvement in practices which reproduce a feminised body, while at the same time consigning the woman to a subjugated identity. The ways in which these processes impact upon different groups of women in terms of class, ethnicity or sexuality is a key focus of concern. However, all studies must return to the issue of choice and conformity. Any time spent conducting empirical research can make the researcher immediately sympathetic to the participants involved. This is sometimes obvious in the work produced, and may be evident in my own study. However, this natural empathy must not be allowed to negate a critical understanding of the practices involved. Spending time with people in their everyday lives can also reinforce the appearance of active individuals bravely making the best of choices available to them. Negrin (2002) systematically interrogates work which emphasises the voluntarism of those involved in cosmetic surgery, or those feminists who see cosmetic procedures as having the potential to challenge established gender identities. She is particularly critical of Kathy Davis' study of women undergoing cosmetic surgery (Davis, 1995). For Davis, the decision to undergo such procedures is a means whereby the woman can bring the physicality of her body into line with her own image of it. In this sense she is using the means available to end her self-estrangement from her body. Cosmetic surgery here becomes a liberating act. Negrin criticises Davis for underplaying the structural constraints on women which lead to the dissatisfaction with their bodies in the first place. Davis is less concerned with structural factors as her emphasis is on the agency of the individuals involved. I can see how it is easy to sympathise with Davis' interpretation. Feminist writers in particular are at pains to grant agency and an astute sense of judgement to the women in their research. However, in dealing with women's use of beauty salons, I believe it is far too limiting to focus our attention solely on women's own experiences as they describe them. This is the tightrope I hope to have walked in taking these experiences and applying a sociological analysis which neither glamorises therapists or clients as pleasure-seeking liberated individuals, nor views them as over-determined ciphers pushed along by social forces beyond their understanding.

Women's (and men's) use of beauty salons leaves unchallenged the socio-economic inequalities inherent in a hierarchical society. Craig (2002) points out that beauty has been used in political terms to reinforce the value of black bodies in a racist culture. Black families in the USA have praised the beauty of their children's dark skin; the civil rights movement coined the term 'Black is beautiful' to promote racial pride; beauty contests for black women have presented a positive view of black female bodies. This is one example of how body practices may be understood in a wider context than individualised and conservative interpretations. However, Craig also shows the limitations of these actions, and how the use of beauty also reinforces particular gender and class hierarchies. In 1968 when women's liberationists were protesting against the Miss America contest, close by the National Association for the Advancement of Coloured People was holding its first Miss Black America Pageant. However, Craig gives the example of Bonnie Allen, one of the few black women participating at the anti-Miss America protest. She expressed the ambiguity of her position in being against the objectivisation of women, while also being in favour of promoting positive images of black women, the aim of the Miss Black America Pageant (Craig, 2002, pp. 4–5).

In her study of Ann Summers parties, Storr (2003) finds much that is valuable in the sexual openness and camaraderie among the woman participants. However, she is also careful to point out how such practices reinforce a normative heterosexuality which leaves homophobia unchallenged:

> Whilst I have been researching and writing this book my friends and colleagues have often asked me whether I think Ann Summers 'a good thing or a bad thing'. I hope it is clear by now that this question is too narrow and simplistic to encompass the complexities of either female homosociality in general or Ann Summers in particular. During my fieldwork, while I was spending my days and evenings with party-goers, they all made it abundantly clear to me in word and deed that they were there 'to have a laugh' above all else. Ann Summers *is* a space in which 'the girls' can take pleasure in the simple fact of being heterosexual women. . . . In the different 'games' being played in Ann Summers, from power games to orgasm bingo, women can have a lot of fun. The problem is that they can have their fun only on the condition that they are willing and able to follow the rules – which, after all, is not a bad metaphor for women's pleasure in heterosexuality more generally.
>
> (Storr, 2003, p. 222)

I agree with Storr's reluctance to see the subject of her study as either 'a good thing or a bad thing'. Beauty salons can be both. They are certainly places where women, and men, can recuperate, socialise, and use to make their lives outside of the salon that little bit easier. The rule following Storr describes may result in the by-products of either pleasure or recognition. Rules may not be agreed with fully, or may be subtly subverted, even while engaging in apparently conformist practices. Of course this rule following is not necessarily recognised as such. This is the value of Bourdieu's use of symbolic violence – what he calls a 'gentle violence' (Bourdieu, 2001, p. 1) where femininity becomes a default position actively sought out by the women on whom it has been imposed. The world of the beauty salon is not about beauty. We are not really ever judged according to aesthetics, but rather aesthetic symbols become signifiers of other categories. Their value is read in classed, racialised, gendered and sexualised terms. The appropriate gender performance achieved through the use of beauty salon treatments may be read as beauty, especially in a highly visual culture operating in the context of liberal individualism. However, it may be more useful to understand salons as producing a range of experiences in relation to gender, culture and pleasure.

Bibliography

Adkins, L. (1995) *Gendered Work: Sexuality, Family and the Labour Market*, Milton Keynes: Open University Press.

—— (2001) 'Cultural Feminization: "Money, Sex and Power" for Women', *Signs*, 26, 3: 669–695.

Adkins, L. and Lury, C. (1999) 'The Labour of Identity: Performing Identities, Performing Economies', *Economy and Society*, 28, 4: 598–614.

—— (2000) 'Making Bodies, Making People, Making Work', in L. McKie and N. Watson (eds) *Organizing Bodies: Policy, Institution and Work*, Basingstoke: Macmillan.

Allsop, J. and Saks, M. (eds) (2002) *Regulating the Health Professions*, London: Sage.

Armstrong, D. (1995) 'The Rise of Surveillance Medicine', *Sociology of Health and Illness*, 17, 3: 393–404.

Averett, S. and Korenman, S. (1995) 'The Economic Reality of *The Beauty Myth*', *The Journal of Human Resources*, 31, 2: 304–330.

Banim, M., Gillen, K. and Guy, A. (2002) 'Escaping the Everyday? Women's Clothing on Holiday', *Everyday Cultures Working Papers No. 6*, Milton Keynes: Open University Press.

Bartky, S. L. (1997) *Femininity and Domination: Studies in the Phenomenology of Oppression*, London: Routledge.

Basow, S. A. (1991) 'The Hairless Ideal: Women and their Body Hair', *Psychology of Women Quarterly*, 15: 83–96.

Beattie, A., Gott, M., Jones, L. and Sidell, M. (eds) (1993) *Health and Well-being: A Reader*, Basingstoke: Open University Press and Macmillan.

Beck, U. (1992) *Risk Society: Towards a New Modernity*, London: Sage.

Bhavani, K. (1997) 'Women's Studies and its Interconnection with "Race", Ethnicity and Sexuality', in V. Robinson and D. Richardson (eds) *Introducing Women's Studies (2nd edn)*, Basingstoke: Palgrave.

Black, P. (2002) '"Ordinary People Come Through Here": Locating the Beauty Salon in Women's Lives', *Feminist Review*, 71: 2–17.

Black, P. and Sharma, U. (2001) 'Men are Real, Women are "Made Up": Beauty Therapy and the Construction of Femininity', *Sociological Review*, 49: 100–116.

Blaxter, M. (1990) *Health and Lifestyles*, London: Routledge.

Bourdieu, P. (1984) *Distinction: A Social Critique of the Judgement of Taste*, London: Routledge.

—— (1990) *The Logic of Practice*, Cambridge: Polity Press.

—— (1993) *Sociology in Question*, London: Sage.

—— (1998) *Practical Reason: On the Theory of Action*, Cambridge: Polity Press.

—— (2001) *Masculine Domination*, Cambridge: Polity Press.

Boyd, R. L. (1996) 'The Great Migration To The North and the Rise of Ethnic Niches for African-American Women in Beauty Culture and Hairdressing, 1910–1920', *Sociological Focus*, 29, 1: 33–45.

Brand, P. Z. (ed.) (2000) *Beauty Matters*, Bloomington: Indiana University Press.

Budd, S. and Sharma, U. (eds) (1994) *The Healing Bond: The Patient–Practitioner Relationship and Therapeutic Responsibility*, London: Routledge.

Butler, J. (1990) *Gender Trouble: Feminism and the Subversion of Identity*, London: Routledge.

—— (1993) *Bodies that Matter: On the Discursive Limits of 'Sex'*, London: Routledge.

—— (1995) 'The Debate Over the Middle Classes', in T. Butler and M. Savage (eds) *Social Change and the Middle Classes*, London: UCL Press.

Calnan, M. (1994) '"Lifestyle" and its Social Meaning', *Advances in Medical Sociology*, 4: 69–78.

Cant, S. and Calnan, M. (1991) 'On the Margins of the Medical Marketplace? An Exploratory Study of Alternative Practitioners' Perceptions', *Sociology of Health and Illness*, 13: 34–51.

Cant, S. and Sharma, U. (1995) 'The Reluctant Profession – Homeopathy and the Search for Legitimacy', *Work, Employment and Society*, 9, 4: 743–762.

—— (1996) 'Demarcation and Transformation Within Homeopathic Knowledge: A Strategy of Professionalization', *Social Science Medicine*, 42, 4: 579–588.

Chapkis, W. (1986) *Beauty Secrets: Women and the Politics of Appearance*, London: The Women's Press.

Cohen, C. B., Stoeltje, B. and Wilk, R. R. (eds) (1995) *Beauty Queens on the Global Stage: Gender, Contests, and Power*, London: Routledge.

Connell, R. W. (1995) *Masculinities*, Cambridge: Polity Press.

Craig, M. L. (2002) *Ain't I a Beauty Queen? Black Women, Beauty, and the Politics of Race,* Oxford: Oxford University Press.

Craik, J. (1994) *The Face of Fashion: Cultural Studies in Fashion*, London: Routledge.

Crawford, R. (1980) 'Healthism and the Medicalization of Everyday Life', *International Journal of Health Services*, 10, 3: 365–387.

Crossley, N. (2001) *The Social Body: Habit, Identity and Desire*, London: Sage.

Davies, C. and Rosser, J. (1986) 'Gendered Jobs in the Health Service: A Problem for Labour Process Analysis', in D. Knights and H. Wilmott (eds) *Gender and the Labour Process*, Aldershot: Gower.

Davis, K. (1991) 'Re-making the She Devil: A Critical Look at Feminist Approaches to Beauty', *Hypatia*, 6, 2: 21–43.

—— (1995) *Reshaping the Female Body: The Dilemma of Cosmetic Surgery*, London: Routledge.

Doane, M. A. (1987) *The Desire to Desire: The Woman's Film of the 1940s*, Basingstoke: Macmillan.

Ehrenreich, B. and Hochschild, A. R. (2003) *Global Woman: Nannies, Maids and Sex Workers in the New Economy*, London: Granta.

Fagan, C. (2002) 'How Many Hours? Work Time Regimes and Preferences in European Countries', in G. Crow and S. Heath (eds) *Social Conceptions of Time – Structure and Process in Work and Everyday Life*, Basingstoke: Palgrave.

Featherstone, M. (1982) 'The Body in Consumer Culture', *Theory, Culture and Society*, 1, 2: 18–33.

—— (1991) *Consumer Culture and Postmodernism*, London: Sage.

Fine, G. (1996) 'Justifying Work: Occupational Rhetorics in Restaurant Kitchens', *Administrative Science Quarterly*, 41: 90–112.

Fineman, S. (ed.) (1993) *Emotion in Organizations*, London: Sage.

Foucaalt, M. (1990) [1984] *The Care of the Self, The History of Sexuality: Volume Three*, London: Penguin.

—— (1991) [1973] *The Birth of the Clinic: An Archaeology of Medical Perception*, London: Routledge.

Freidson, E. (1970) *Profession of Medicine: A Study of the Sociology of Applied Knowledge*, London: University of Chicago Press.

Friedan, B. (1963) *The Feminine Mystique*, Harmondsworth: Penguin.

Furman, F. K. (1997) *Facing the Mirror: Older Women and Beauty Shop Culture*, London: Routledge.

Gates, H. L. and Oliver, T. H. (eds) (1999) *W. E. B. Du Bois: The Souls of Black Folk*, New York: W. W. Norton.

Gavron, H. (1966) *The Captive Wife: Conflicts of Housebound Mothers*, London: Routledge & Kegan Paul.

Gilman, S. L. (1999) *Making the Body Beautiful: A Cultural History of Aesthetic Surgery*, Oxford: Princeton University Press.

Gimlin, D. (1996) 'Pamela's Place: Power and Negotiation in the Hair Salon', *Gender and Society*, 10: 505–526.

—— (2002) *Body Work: Beauty and Self-Image in American Culture*, London: University of California Press.

Grosz, E. (1994) *Volatile Bodies: Toward a Corporeal Feminism*, Bloomington: Indiana University Press.

Guild News (1999) 'Beauty Index 1999', *Journal of the Guild of Professional Beauty Therapists*, January/February.

—— (2001) 'Beauty Index 2001', *Journal of the Guild of Professional Beauty Therapists*.

—— (2002) 'Beauty Index 2003', *Journal of the Guild of Professional Beauty Therapists*, December.

Haiken, E. (1997) *Venus Envy: A History of Cosmetic Surgery*, London: Johns Hopkins University Press.

Hamermesh, D. S. and Biddle, J. E. (1994) 'Beauty and the Labour Market', *The American Economic Review*, 84, 5: 1174–1194.

Harding, S. (1991) *Whose Science? Whose Knowledge? Thinking From Women's Lives*, Milton Keynes: Open University Press.

Health Education Unit, World Health Organisation (1993) *Lifestyles and Health*, in Beattie *et al.*, *op cit.*

Herzig, R. (1999) 'Removing Roots: "North American Hiroshima Maidens" and the X Ray', *Technology and Culture*, 40, 4: 723–745.

Hochschild, A. (1983) *The Managed Heart: Commercialization of Human Feeling*, Berkley: University of California Press.

Holland, J., Ramazanoglu, C., Sharpe, S. and Thomson, R. (1994) 'Power and Desire: The Embodiment of Female Sexuality', *Feminist Review*, 46: 21–38.

Hollands, R. G. (1995) *Friday Night, Saturday Night: Youth Cultural Identi-fication in the Post-Industrial City*, Newcastle: University of Newcastle.

hooks, b. (1982) *Ain't I a Woman: Black Women and Feminism*, London: Pluto Press.

Illich, I. (1975) *Medical Nemesis*, London: Calder and Boyars.

Jeffries, S. (1997) *The Idea of Prostitution*, Melbourne: Spinfex.

Jenson, J., Hagen, E. and Reddy, C. (1988) *Feminization of the Labour Force: Paradoxes and Promises*, Cambridge: Polity Press.

Katz, C. and Monk, J. (eds) (1993) *Full Circles: Geographies of Women Over the Life Course*, London: Routledge.

Krais, B. (1993) 'Gender and Symbolic Violence: Female Oppression in the Light of Pierre Bourdieu's Theory of Social Practice', in C. Calhoun, E. LiPuma and M. Postone (eds) *Bourdieu: Critical Perspectives*, Cambridge: Polity Press.

Kyle, D. J. and Mahler, H. I. M. (1996) 'The Effects of Hair Color and Cosmetic Use on Perception of a Female's Ability', *Psychology of Women Quarterly*, 20: 447–455.

Lash, S. and Urry, J. (1994) *Economies of Signs and Space*, London: Sage.

Lawler, S. (1999) ' "Getting Out and Getting Away": Women's Narratives of Class Mobility', *Feminist Review*, 63: 3–24.

Lawson, H., M. (1999) 'Working on Hair', *Qualitative Sociology*, 22, 3: 235–257.

Lofland, L. H. (1976) 'The "Thereness" of Women: A Selective Review of Urban Sociology', in M. Millman and R. M. Kanter *Another Voice: Feminist Perspectives on Social Life and Social Science*, New York: Octagon Books.

Lovell, T. (2000) 'Thinking Feminism With and Against Bourdieu', *Feminist Theory*, 1, 1: 11–32.

Lupton, D. (1994) *Medicine as Culture: Illness, Disease and the Body in Western Societies*, London: Sage.

—— (1995) *The Imperative of Health: Public Health and the Regulated Body*, London: Sage.

—— (1997) 'Foucault and the Medicalisation Critique', in A. Petersen and R. Bunton (eds) *Foucault, Health and Medicine*, London: Routledge.

Lury, C. (1997) *Consumer Culture*, Cambridge: Polity Press.

MacCannell, D. and MacCannell, J. F. (1987) 'The Beauty System', in N. Armstrong and L. Tannenhouse (eds) *The Ideology of Conduct: Essays on the Literature and the History of Sexuality*, London: Methuen.

McClintock, A. (1995) *Imperial Leather: Race, Gender and Sexuality in the Colonial Contest*, London: Routledge.

McRobbie, A. (1991) *Feminism and Youth Culture: From Jackie to Just Seventeen*, London: Macmillan.

Massey, D. (1984) *Spatial Divisions of Labour: Social Structures and the Geography of Production*, Basingstoke: Macmillan.

—— (1994) *Space, Place and Gender*, Cambridge: Polity Press.

Mauss, M. (1973) 'Techniques of the Body', *Economy and Society*, 2, 1: 70–88.

Meikle, J. (2003) 'NHS Tells Patients to Change Lifestyle', *Guardian*, 24 July, p. 9.

Mills, C. W. (1967) [1959] *The Sociological Imagination*, Oxford: Oxford University Press.

Moseley, R. and Read, J. (2002) '"Having it Ally": Popular Television (Post-) Feminism', *Feminist Media Studies*, 2, 2: 231–249.

Mottier, V. (2002) 'Masculine Domination: Gender and Power in Bourdieu's Writings', *Feminist Theory*, 3, 3: 345–359.

Nava, M. (1998) 'The Cosmopolitanism of Commerce and the Allure of Difference: Selfridges, the Russian Ballet and the Tango', *International Journal of Cultural Studies*, 1, 2: 163–196.

Negrin, L. (2002) 'Cosmetic Surgery and the Eclipse of Identity', *Body and Society*, 8, 4: 21–42.

Nettleton, S. (1995) *The Sociology of Health and Illness*, Cambridge: Polity Press.

—— (1997) 'Governing the Risky Self: How to Become Healthy, Wealthy and Wise', in P. Petersen and R. Bunton (eds) *Foucault, Health and Medicine*, London: Routledge.

Newton, T. (1995) *"Managing' Stress: Emotion and Power at Work*, London: Sage.

Offe, C. (1985) *Disorganised Capitalism: Contemporary Transformations of Work Politics*, Cambridge: Polity Press.

Oldenburg, R. and Hummon, D. M. (1991) 'The Great Good Place: Cafes, Coffee Shops, Community Centers, Beauty Parlours, General Stores, Bars, Hangouts, and How They Get You Through The Day', *Social Forces,* 69, 3: 931.

O'Neill, G. (1993) *A Night Out With The Girls: Women Having a Good Time*, London: The Women's Press.

Oullette, L. (1999) 'Inventing the Cosmo Girl: Class Identity and Girl-style American Dreams', *Media, Culture and Society*, 21, 359–383.

Passerini, L. (1989) 'Women's Personal Narratives: Myths, Experiences and Emotions', in The Personal Narratives Group (eds) *Interpreting Women's Lives: Feminist Theory and Personal Narratives*, Bloomington: Indiana University Press.

Peiss, K. (1998) *Hope in a Jar: The Making of America's Beauty Culture*, New York: Metropolitan Books.

Pirie, Z. (2003) 'Impact of Delivering Shiatsu in a General Practice', Unpublished Ph.D. thesis, University of Sheffield.

Radner, H. (1989) '"This Time's For Me": Making Up and Feminine Practice', *Cultural Studies*, 3, 3: 301–322.

Ramazanoglu, C. (ed.) (1993) *Up Against Foucault: Explorations of Some Tensions Between Foucault and Feminism*, London: Routledge.

Rooks, N. L. (1998)*Hair Raising: Beauty, Culture, and African-American Women*, London: Rutgers University Press.

Rose, J. (1983) 'Femininity and its Discontents', *Feminist Review*, 14: 5–21.

Rose, N. (1999) [1989] *Governing the Soul: The Shaping of the Private Self*, London: Free Association Books.

Rosenthal, G. (1992) 'A Biographical Case Study of a Victimizer's Daughter', *Journal of Narrative and Life History*, 2, 2: 105–127.

Rowbotham, S. (1997) *A Century of Women*, Harmondsworth: Penguin.

Saltonstall, R. (1993) 'Healthy Bodies, Social Bodies: Men's and Women's Concepts and Practices of Health in Everyday Life', *Social Science Medicine*, 36, 1: 7–14.

Savage, M., Barlow, B., Dickens, P. and Fielding, T. (1992) *Property, Bureaucracy and Culture: Middle-Class Formation in Contemporary Britain*, London: Routledge.

Scott-Heron, G. (1989) [1970] 'Brother', *The Revolution Will Not Be Televised*, Bluebird Records, BMG Music International.

Sharma, U. (1994) 'The Equation of Responsibility: Complementary Practitioners and Their Patients', in Budd and Sharma (eds) *op cit.*

—— (1995) *Complementary Medicine Today: Practitioners and Patients*, London: Routledge.

Sharma, U. and Black, P. (1999) *The Sociology of Pampering: Beauty Therapy as a Form of Work*, Centre for Social Research, University of Derby, Working Papers Series.

—— (2001) 'Look Good Feel Better: Beauty Therapy as Emotional Labour', *Sociology*, 35, 4: 913–931.

Shields, R. (1990) 'The "System of Pleasure": Liminality and the Carnivalesque at Brighton', *Theory, Culture and Society*, 7: 39–72.

Skeggs, B. (2001) 'The Toilet Paper: Femininity, Class and Misrecognition', *Women's Studies International Forum*, 24, 3 and 4: 295–307.

—— (1997) *Formations of Class and Gender: Becoming Respectable*, London: Sage.

Smith, D. (1987) *The Everyday World as Problematic: A Feminist Sociology*, Oxford: Alden Press.

Smith, P. (1992) *The Emotional Labour of Nursing*, Basingstoke: Macmillan.

Southerton, D., Shove, E. and Warde, A. (2001) "Harried and Hurried': Time Shortage and the Co-ordination of Everyday Life', CRIC Discussion Paper 47, Centre for Research on Innovation and Competition, Manchester: University of Manchester and UMIST.

Stacey, J. (1994) *Star Gazing: Hollywood Cinema and Female Spectatorship*, London: Routledge.

—— (1997) 'Untangling Feminist Theory', in D. Richardson and V. Robinson, *op cit.*

Sparke, P. (1995) *As Long as it's Pink: The Sexual Politics of Taste*, London: Pandora.

Storr, M. (2003) *Latex and Lingerie: Shopping for Pleasure at Ann Summers Parties*, Oxford: Berg.

Synnott, A. (1987) 'Shame and Glory: A Sociology of Hair', *The British Journal of Sociology*, 38, 3: 381–413.

—— (1990) 'Truth and Goodness, Mirrors and Masks – Part II – A Sociology of Beauty and the Face', *British Journal of Sociology*, 41, 1: 55–76.

—— (1993) *The Body Social: Symbolism, Self and Society*, London: Routledge.

Thompson, J. (1998) 'The Politics of Hair in Kathmandu, Nepal', *Asian Journal of Women's Studies,* 4, 1: 77–129.

Tiggerman, M. and Kenyon, S. J. (1998) 'The Hairless Norm: The Removal of Body Hair in Women', *Sex Roles*, 39, 11/12: 873–885.

Tomlinson, M. (2003) 'Lifestyle and Social Class', *European Sociological Review*, 19, 1: 97–111.

Treweek, G. L. (1996) 'Emotion Work, Order, and Emotional Power in Care Assistant Work', in V. James and J. Gabe (eds) *Health and the Sociology of Emotions*, Oxford: Blackwell.

Turner, B. (1996) *The Body and Society: Explorations in Social Theory (2nd edn)*, London: Sage.

Tyler, M. and Abbott, P. (1998) 'Chocs Away: Weight Watching in the Contemporary Airline Industry', *Sociology*, 32, 3: 433–450.

Tyler, M. and Hancock, P. (2001) 'Flight Attendants and the Management of Gendered "Organizational Bodies"', in K. Backett-Milburn and L. McKie (eds) *Constructing Gendered Bodies*, Basingstoke: Palgrave.

Walkerdine, V. (1997) *Daddy's Girl: Young Girls and Popular Culture*, London: Routledge.

Webster, M. and Driskell, J. E. (1983) 'Beauty as Status', *American Journal of Sociology*, 89, 1: 140–165.

Weekes, D. (1997) 'Shades of Blackness: Young Female Constructions of Beauty', in H. S. Mirza (ed.) *Black British Feminism*, London: Routledge.

Wellington, C. A. and Bryson, J. R. (2001) 'At Face Value? Image Consultancy, Emotional Labour and Professional Work', *Sociology*, 35, 4: 933–946.

Wharton, A. (1993) 'The Affective Consequences of Service Work: Managing Emotions on the Job', *Work and Occupations*, 20: 205–232.

Willett, J. A. (2000) *Permanent Waves: The Making of the American Beauty Shop*, London: New York University Press.

Winship, J. (1987) *Inside Women's Magazines*, London: Pandora Press.

Witz, A. (1992) *Professions and Patriarchy*, London: Routledge.

—— (2000) 'Whose Body Matters? Feminist Sociology and the Corporeal Turn in Sociology and Feminism', *Body and Society*, 6, 2: 1–24.

Witz, A., Warhurst, C. and Nickson, D. (2003) 'The Labour of Aesthetics and the Aesthetics of Organization', *Organization*, 10, 1: 33–54.

Wolf, N. (1990) *The Beauty Myth: How Images of Beauty are Used Against Women*, London: Vintage.

Young, A. (1980) 'The Discourse of Stress and the Reproduction of Conventional Knowledge', *Social Science and Medicine*, 14B: 133–146.

Young, I. (1980) 'Throwing Like a Girl', *Human Studies*, 3: 137–156.

Zdatny, S. (1993) 'Fashion and Class Struggle: The Case of *Coiffure*', *Social History*, 18, 1: 53–72.

Index